COOKING

WITHOUT NO-NOs

with

Nutritional Information
For the Health Conscious

★ Low Cholesterol

★ Low Saturated Fats

★ No Refined Sugar

★ No Caffeine

★ Low Sodium

TABLE OF CONTENTS

Preface 1
Dedication 3
Nutritional Information 4
How Recipes Are Analyzed 4
Food Groups 4
Calculating Fat Percentage in Food 5
What Labels Really Mean 7
Helpful Hints 10
Weights and Measures 13
Sugar Equivalents 14
Powdered Sugar Replacement 14
Flour Equivalents 15
Substitutions 16
Homemade Egg Substitute 16
Products Used 17
Sample Menus 19

APPETIZERS and SNACKS 23

VEGETABLES, SALADS, and DRESSINGS 39

ENTREES 57

DESSERTS 91

CAKES 109

PIES 121

COOKIES 133

BREAKFASTS 141

EGGS and CHEESE 149

BREAD and MUFFINS 161

BEVERAGES 177

INDEX 193

FOREWORD

Congratulations on having chosen a wonderful addition to your cookbook library. It is chock full of helpful hints, interesting tidbits and great recipes! But above all, it provides the nutrient analysis data which allows you to see exactly how much of each nutritional component you'll be adding to your diet. This kind of accuracy is very much needed for individualizing any restrictions of total calories.

In my work, primarily with diabetics and those involved in weight management, I continually find much confusion about the relative importance of fat, sugar and calories. While limiting concentrated sugar is the primary concern of a diabetic, fat and calories must be modified to meet the particular lifestyle needs and medical history of each person. In weight management, fat becomes the focal point of concern. With the information provided here, the recipes can be used and enjoyed by everyone.

I am truly delighted with the variety of recipes, the completeness of the dietary analysis and the useful suggestions from one who has learned to cook in this special way.

Juli Hunter, M.S., R.D.
Nutritional Consultant
Phoenix, AZ

CONSULT YOUR DOCTOR, DIETITIAN or NUTRITIONIST

This book was not intended to replace medical advice. Consult your doctor or professional before changing your diet.

The sample menus are based on approximately 1200 calories per day. This amount of calories may not be sufficient for children, pregnant or lactating women, and/or other medical conditions.

PREFACE

This collection of recipes started when I decided to lose weight and also eliminate table sugar, salt, caffeine and saturated fats from my diet for health reasons. At about the same time, my husband was diagnosed as having diabetes (Type II), so he also had to make changes to a healthier food regime. This involved a lot of research about food and the various food groups.

It has long been my opinion that not enough nutritional information has been available. Many recipes state that they are "low" in fats, sodium, cholesterol, etc. but one never knows what that actually means.

Without the detailed nutritional information, it is very difficult for an individual to know what he is consuming.

After learning how to figure the nutritional information manually, I talked to several nutritionists about my ideas and they were very receptive. They also suggested that I use computerized software to do the analysis. The one I chose uses the latest information and guidelines published by the USDA and American Diabetic Association (ADA), and offers updates periodically.

The food exchanges listed in the nutritional information are the basic diabetic exchanges which are also utilized by many weight loss programs.

Foods that have approximately the same amount of calories, protein, carbohydrate and fat are known as Food Exchanges/ Groups. A Food Exchange is one item from the Food Group or list. These food lists are available from physicians, nutritionists and the ADA.

Some recipes are modified family favorites, friends requests to convert a favorite, others collected from many sources and some are the result of my own imagination and experimentation.

I hope you enjoy this cookbook whether you are trying to lose weight, or just want to try something different.

Edith Nader

DEDICATION

This book is dedicated to my husband — Bill, who suffered through all my trials and experimentations with recipes and has always given me support in my endeavors.

NUTRITIONAL INFORMATION

Every recipe contains nutritional information. The calorie count of an individual serving of the recipe and the amount (in grams or milligrams), of protein (pro), carbohydrates (carb), fat, saturated fat (satfat), cholesterol (chol) and sodium (sod) are listed.

Food exchanges (ADA as of Jan. 1990) are listed as protein (pro), vegetable (veg), bread (brd), fat, milk and fruit (frt).

The percent of calories per serving of total fat and saturated fat are listed.

HOW RECIPES ARE ANALYZED

- When there are ingredient choices in a recipe, the first ingredient listed is used for the analysis
- Optional ingredients are omitted
- Analysis for all recipes was done on an IBM PC using software recognized by dietitions.

The primary data sources are the USDA Handbooks #8-1 through #8-21. Other USDA sources and other reliable data were used when the previously mentioned did not include necessary information.

FOOD GROUPS

The four basic food groups are: (1) Milk, (2) Meat or Protein, (3) Fruits and Vegetables, and (4) Grains or Starch/Bread. Additional food groups are Combination Foods and Other.

Milk consists of milk, yogurt, cheese, cottage cheese, ice cream, ice milk and frozen yogurt.

Meat or Protein consists of lean meat, fish, poultry, eggs, dried peas and beans, peanut butter, nuts and seeds.

Fruit-Vegetable consists of juices, fresh and dried fruit, and vegetables.

Grains consist of breads, cereal, pasta, rice, grits, tortillas, rolls and muffins.

Combination Foods are soup, macaroni and cheese, stews, casseroles, pizza, sandwiches, etc. which are servings from the basic four food groups.

Other category consists of fats, cookies, cakes, jelly, potato chips, soft drinks, etc. which have no recommended number of servings.

The following table contains the minimum recommended number of servings based on 1200 calories per day:

Age	Milk	Meat Protein	Fruit Veg	Grains
1-10	3	2	4	4
11-18	4	2	4	4
Adults	2	2	4	4
Preg women	4	3	4	4

CALCULATING THE PERCENTAGE OF FAT IN FOODS

The steps listed below are necessary to calculate the percentage of fat in foods. A meal plan should contain less than 25% to 30% of the total calories from fat.

It is appropriate to apply this formula to prepared meals (i.e., TV dinners) or to snack foods such as crackers, chips, cookies, pudding, frozen desserts, etc.

It is not always appropriate to calculate the percentage of fat in meat and cheese since they are generally higher than 30% fat. Naturally, you must choose lean meats and low-fat dairy products. This formula should not be applied to margarine or oils since they are in fact, "fats".

Steps:

1)   1 gram of fat = 9 calories

2)   Multiply the number of grams of fat in the product by 9

      11 grams of fat X 9 calories per gram = 99 calories from fat

3)   Divide the calories from fat by the total calories in the product

$$\frac{99 \text{ calories from fat}}{200 \text{ calorie product}} = 50\% \text{ fat (too high)}$$

A simplified way of insuring that a product has less than 30% of its calories from fat (without doing the above calculation) is to choose foods that contain 3 grams of fat or less per 100 calories.

      A 300 calorie microwaveable dinner should contain 9 grams of fat or less.

If you wish to calculate the percentage of protein, carbohydrate or alcohol in foods, substitute the following into step 1:

      1 gram protein = 4 calories
      1 gram carbohydrate = 4 calories
      1 gram alcohol = 7 calories

When evaluating products for their fat content, remember to check the serving size.

WHAT LABELS REALLY MEAN

According to the current law, the ingredients in most foods must be listed on the package. The ingredient with the largest amount is listed first, followed by the other ingredients in descending order by weight. Additives must also be listed. However, the label may state "artificial coloring" or "artificial flavoring". It is not necessary to state exactly what they are.

If you have specific questions on a product, write to the company — they are usually most helpful, some have a toll free telephone number on the product.

Another label to watch is "juice" versus "drink". "Juice" is probably pure juice where "drink" contains some juice.

IMITATION

This label means that the product MAY not be as nutritious as the one it is "imitating". However, some of these products are just as nutritious.

LOW-CALORIE

Under the FDA regulations, foods that contain 40 calories or less per single serving, or less than .4 calories per gram may be labeled "low-calorie".

REDUCED CALORIE

This label must list the number of calories in the product versus the number of calories in the unmodified product. If a product or food is naturally low in calories, such as some vegetables (i.e., green beans), it cannot be labeled "low calorie" as that would infer that these green beans are lower in calories than any other green beans.

LITE / LIGHT

This label has more than one definition. It may mean that the product has fewer calories, that the product has less sodium, less sugar, less density or less fat. Read this label carefully.

SUGAR-FREE

This label means that the product does not contain "sugar", but that does not mean it is lower in calories. Check the label to note if the item can be used for weight control. Corn syrup and ingredients that end in "ose" i.e. sucrose and fructose, are also types of sugar.

NUTRITION INFORMATION

The FDA requires that any food containing additives or stating nutritional claims, must have the nutritional information on the label. This includes "low" and "reduced" calorie products.

Nutrition information includes the total number of servings in the product and the size of a single serving. Single serving information includes the number of calories and, the amounts of protein, carbohydrates and fats. The USRDA's (U.S. Recommended Dietary Allowances) of protein and seven vitamins and minerals in a single serving must be listed. These are vitamins A and C, thiamine, riboflavin, niacin, calcium and iron.

The FDA developed the RDA's to provide guidelines for the amount of vitamins and minerals an individual needs each day to stay healthy. However, each individuals needs may vary. Most RDA's exceed minimum requirements. The RDA's listed are for healthy people.

The FDA currently does not have a legal definition for the words "natural, organic or health" food. Read the label carefully to determine which ingredient(s) are actually in these categories.

SODIUM DEFINITIONS

Amounts of sodium per serving:
    Sodium Free — less than 5 mg
    Very Low-Sodium — no more than 35mg
    Low-Sodium — no more than 140mg
    Reduced Sodium — sodium content reduced by 75% (label must show before and after)
    Unsalted, Without Salt Added, No Salt Added — salt was not added to a product that is normally prepared with salt. Label must still show sodium content per serving.

MEAT and POULTRY DEFINITIONS

Effective March 1987, the USDA requirements are as follows:

Extra Lean — no more than 5% fat
Lean and LowFat — less than 10% fat
Light, Lite, Leaner and Lower Fat — contains at least 25% less fat than the majority of comparable products.

FATS

SATURATED fat — a fat that is usually solid or semi-solid at room temperature.

POLYUNSATURATED fat — vegetable oil (safflower, corn, canola, etc.)

HYDROGENATED, PARTIALLY HYDROGENATED — use caution. A hydrogenated fat is one that has been changed to a solid.

Peanut butter is a good example — if the oil separates at room temperature, it is not hydrogenated. Naturally ground peanut butter needs to be refrigerated to help prevent oil separation.

EXAMPLE — if a product containing fat is thick or solid at room temperature, it is an unhealthy fat.

HELPFUL HINTS

To improve the flavor of onion in many dishes, grate the onion instead of chopped or diced, make sure there are no pieces to bite into. Especially good for meat loaf, egg or tuna salad.

•

For tastier rice or pasta, add a Sodium Free chicken bullion cube to the cooking water.

•

If only half of a frozen food package is needed, the whole package needn't be thawed. Run very hot water over a sharp knife and cut the package in half. Wrap the remaining portion in aluminum foil and return it to the freezer.

•

To help keep skinned chicken moist when baking, spray the chicken with a release agent (such as Pam) before cooking and half way through cooking time.

•

When grinding food that isn't going to be used right away, put a rubber band around the neck of a plastic bag to hold it on the food grinder opening — the food falls neatly into the bag and is ready for storage.

•

Be sure salad greens are thoroughly dry before adding the dressing. The dressing won't cling to wet greens and the moisture dilutes it as well.

•

To core an apple — cut the apple in half and use the small end of a melon baller to carve out the seeds. Use a knife to cut away the stem. This is neater and less waste.

•

Egg whites should be at room temperature for beating to attain maximum volume.

•

Eggs separate easier when cold.

•

Roll cookie or pie dough between two sheets of wax paper. If dough gets warm, slip it on to a baking sheet and place in freezer for a few minutes.

•

Store leftover heels/slices of bread in the freezer to use whenever bread crumbs are needed. Grate into crumbs using the coarse side of a grater. Crumbs can also be made by putting fresh bread in the blender for a few seconds.

•

When preparing food or baking, fill the dish pan with hot soapy water. Put all utensils, dishes, bowls, etc. in the soapy water as soon as finished. The food doesn't get dried on and you don't get all those "extra" tasting calories.

•

To prevent scratching or marring of counter tops when mixing in a bowl or pan, put a paper towel under the bowl, it will turn easier too.

•

To clean the blades of the blender, add a little warm soapy water to the blender and "blend" a few seconds.

•

When using melted reduced calorie margarine, it may look curdled after some ingredients are added. It will bind again after flour, etc. is added.

•

For a drop or two of fresh lemon juice, poke a toothpick through the skin and squeeze out what you need.

•

To cut an onion without crying, place it in the freezer about 20 minutes before slicing.

•

When serving soft foods such as eggplant, use a spatula to prevent breaking.

•

To remove the white membrane from oranges for use in fancy desserts or salads, soak the orange in boiling water for 5 minutes before peeling.

•

To drain canned fruit or kidney beans, puncture top of can before opening it and invert can in a container to catch the liquid. When the liquid has been drained, open the can and remove the contents.

•

When measuring margarine, etc., dip the spoon in hot water and the item will slip out easier.

•

When a recipe uses both oil and honey, measure the oil first and the honey will come out easier.

•

Use muffin tins sprayed with release agent as molds when baking stuffed green peppers.

•

Add a little milk to the water when cooking cauliflower, and the cauliflower will remain white.

•

Add chopped fruits to flour mixture in recipes, unless specific instructions state otherwise. The fruit will be distributed evener and not clump.

•

When cooking cabbage, place a small tin cup or can half full of vinegar on the stove near the cabbage, and it will absorb the odor.

•

Store dried fruits such as raisins, prunes, dates and apricots in the freezer. They will maintain their freshness better.

•

All dried fruit chop easier after being stored in the freezer. Add a little flour to the fruit while chopping and for storing, this will help prevent sticking of the pieces. Store the chopped dried fruit in the freezer until ready to use.

•

To separate fat from the juices of a roast or poultry, drop ice cubes into the pan after removing the roast. The fat solidifies around the ice cubes and when the cubes are removed, the fat goes with them.

•

To restore crispness to crackers, put them in a 350ºF. oven for 3 to 5 minutes.

•

Quick substitute coffee filter, use white paper towels or white dinner napkins.

WEIGHTS and MEASURES

3 tsp	=	1 tab
4 tab	=	1/4 cup
5 tab +1 tsp	=	1/3 cup
8 tab	=	1/2 cup
10 tab +2 tsp	=	2/3 cup
12 tab	=	3/4 cup
16 tab	=	1 cup
1 cup	=	8 fluid ounces
1 cup	=	1/2 pint
2 cups	=	1 pint
4 cups	=	1 quart
4 quarts	=	1 gallon
8 quarts	=	1 peck
4 pecks	=	1 bushel
16 ounces	=	1 pound
2 cups liquid	=	1 pound
2 cups margarine	=	1 pound
4 cups flour	=	1 pound
1/4 lb margarine	=	1/2 cup
1 lb grated cheese	=	4 cups
8 egg whites	=	1 cup approx
16 egg yolks	=	1 cup approx
juice of 1 lemon	=	2 to 3 tab
1 cup raw macaroni	=	2 cups cooked
1 cup raw rice	=	3-4 cups cooked
1 pkt unflavored gelatin	=	1 tab gelatin
1/2 tsp ginger root	=	1/8 tsp ground ginger

ABBREVIATIONS

tsp	=	teaspoon
tab	=	tablespoon
oz	=	ounce
lb	=	pound
pkt	=	packet
gm	=	gram
mg	=	milligram
<	=	less than

SUGAR EQUIVALENTS

1 cup replacement	=	1 cup sugar
2/3 cup fructose	=	1 cup sugar
1 pkt	=	2 tsp sugar
6 pkts	=	1/4 cup sugar
8 pkts	=	1/3 cup sugar
12 pkts	=	1/2 cup sugar
7/8 cup honey	=	1 cup sugar

BULK SWEET 'N LOW

1 tsp	=	1/4 cup sugar
1-1/3 tsp	=	1/3 cup sugar
2 tsp	=	1/2 cup sugar
4 tsp	=	1 cup sugar

POWDERED SUGAR REPLACEMENT

1 cup nonfat dry milk powder
1 cup cornstarch
1/3 cup granulated fructose
   or 1/2 cup Sugar Twin

Combine all ingredients in blender or food processor. Mix until blended into a powder.

Yield: 2 cups, 1 serving = 1/4 cup.

Serves 8. Each serving provides: 1/2 pro,1/2 milk.

With Fructose — Per serving: 110 cal, 3gm pro, 18gm carb, 0gm fat, 2mg chol, 47mg sod

With Sugar Twin — Per serving: 91 cal, 3gm pro, 19gm carb, 0gm fat, 2mg chol, 47mg sod

FLOUR EQUIVALENTS

The following are equivalents of 1 cup of wheat flour.

 1 cup barley flour
 1 cup corn flour
 3/4 cup coarse corn meal
 1 scant cup fine corn meal
 7/8 cup rice flour
 1-1/4 cups rye flour
 2/3 cup oat flour
 5/8 cup potato flour
 1 cup tapioca flour
 1-1/3 cups soy flour

The following are equivalents of 1 tablespoon of wheat flour for thickening sauces, gravies, puddings, etc.:

 1/2 tab corn starch
 1/2 tab arrowroot
 1/2 tab potato starch flour
 1 tab rice flour
 2 tab quick cooking tapioca

NOTE: When using flours other than wheat, there will be some difference in the texture, moistness and heaviness of the product. Rice flour is bland and has a slightly grainy texture. Soy flour may be used alone in cookies, other products may be better when a blend of flours is used. Soy flour should also be used with eggs in the recipe. When substituting other flours for wheat flour, a better texture is usually obtained by combining flours. The texture of bread and muffins is improved when the dough is allowed to stand in the baking pan for 20 minutes before baking.

SUBSTITUTIONS

1 tab cornstarch	=	2 tab all purpose flour (for thickening)
1 tab fresh herbs	=	1 tsp dried
1 small fresh onion	=	1 tab instant minced onion, dehydrated
1 tsp dry mustard	=	1 tab prepared mustard
1 clove garlic	=	1/8 tsp garlic powder
1 cup tomato juice	=	1/2 cup tomato sauce + 1/2 cup water
1 egg	=	2 egg whites
	=	1/4 cup egg substitute
	=	1 tsp baking powder (for bulk)
Milk	=	water or fruit juice
1 cup liquid	=	16 oz applesauce or 1-1/2 cups mashed bananas
Margarine or shortening	=	mayonnaise

HOMEMADE EGG SUBSTITUTE

6 egg whites
1/4 cup powdered nonfat milk, dry
1 tab unsaturated vegetable oil

Combine all ingredients in mixing bowl and mix until smooth. Store in refrigerator up to 1 week. Freezes well.

Yield: 1 cup, 1/4 cup = 1 egg Serves 4. Each serving provides: 1/2 pro, 1/2 fat. Per serving: 70 cal, 7gm pro, 3gm carb, 3gm fat, 1mg chol, 98mg sod.

PRODUCTS USED

The following products were used in the recipes in this book. These are not the only brands that can be used as the brands may vary in different areas. Be sure to read the labels.

Bread — 40 calories per slice, many varieties available

Carob — unsweetened powder, chips, melting block — available at health food stores i.e., GNC, Magic Mill

Cheese — lowfat (6gm or less of fat per ounce), low-sodium (50 calories per oz) i.e., Lite-Line, Weight Watchers

Chicken Bullion — sodium free i.e., Health Valley, Steero

Cottage Cheese — skim or 1% milkfat (90 calories per 1/2 cup) i.e., Slender, Weight Watchers

Egg Substitute — Eggbeaters, if using another brand, check the label as the nutritional information will vary

Extracts/Flavorings — use ''pure'' if available

Lecithin Liquid — i.e., Fern, available at most health food stores

Margarine — reduced calorie soft, not stick (50 calories per tab) i.e., Blue Bonnet, Fleischmans, Imperial, Mazola, Parkay, Weight Watchers

Mayonnaise — nonfat (12 calorie per tab) i.e., Kraft Free, Weight Watchers

Milk powder dry — instant skim milk (80 calories per 1/3 cup dry) i.e., ALBA, Carnation

Release Agent — i.e., Pam, Vegelene

Salad Dressings — reduced calorie varies from 3 to 20 calories per tab i.e., Good Seasons No Oil, Golden Harvest, Hain, Weight Watchers

Tahini or Sesame Butter — i.e., Sahadi, Phoenicia Brand, available at health food and import stores

Unflavored Gelatin — i.e., KNOX

Vegetable Oil — unsaturated i.e., Wesson, Mazola, Safflower, Canola

Yogurt — low or nonfat i.e., Dannon, Weight Watchers, Yoplait

SAMPLE MENUS
(approximately 1200 calories per day)
*Recipes included

Day 1

Breakfast
    1/2 med. Banana
    3/4 oz cereal
    1 cup skim milk

Lunch
    *Tuna Salad
    1 oz pita bread
    Vegetable sticks
    Small Orange

Dinner
    *Chicken Kabobs
    1/2 cup cooked rice
    1 cup green beans
    1 cup salad
    2 tab low calorie dressing
    1/2 cup Sugar Free Jello

Snack
    *Milkshake

Day 2

Breakfast
    1/2 grapefruit
    *Breakfast Danish
    1/2 cup skim milk

Lunch
    *Chicken Salad
    2 slices bread (40 calorie)
    Vegetable sticks
    Small Apple

Dinner
    *Polynesian Fish
    1/2 cup cooked rice
    1 cup broccoli
    1/2 cup skim milk
    1/2 cup Sugar Free Jello

Snack
    *Mousse

SAMPLE MENUS

(approximately 1200 calories per day)
*Recipes included

Day 3

Breakfast
Small Orange
1/2 cup cooked oatmeal
1/2 cup skim milk

Lunch
2/3 cup lowfat cottage cheese
Vegetable sticks
6 melba rounds
1 cup fresh strawberries

Dinner
*Poached fish
1 cup salad
2 tab low calorie dressing
1 cup broccoli
*Rice Pudding

Snack
*Banana Cooler

Day 4

Breakfast
1/2 grapefruit
3/4 oz cereal
1 cup skim milk

Lunch
Stuffed Tomato
*Tuna Salad
Vegetable Sticks
1 slice bread (40 calorie)
Small Apple

Dinner
*Eggplant Italian Style
1 cup salad
2 tab low calorie dressing
*4 Oatmeal cookies

Snack
*Mousse

SAMPLE MENUS
(approximately 1200 calories per day)
*Recipes included

Day 5

Breakfast	1/2 cup sliced peaches *Tofu for Breakfast 1 slice toast (40 calorie) 1 tsp margarine
Lunch	*Garbanzo Burger 1 oz pita bread Vegetable sticks Small Apple
Dinner	*Turkey Divan *Spinach Puffs 1 cup salad 2 tab low calorie dressing 1 slice bread (40 calorie) *Dreamy Fruit
Snack	*Milkshake

Day 6

Breakfast	Small Orange 1 oz low fat cheese melted on toast (40 calorie) 1 cup skim milk
Lunch	Chefs Salad 3 cups veggies 2 oz turkey 2 tab low calorie dressing 5 melba rounds Small Apple
Dinner	*Tofu Stir Fry 1 cup steamed broccoli 1 slice bread (40 calorie) *Brownie
Snack	*Strawberry Cooler

SAMPLE MENUS
(approximately 1200 calories per day)
*Recipes included

Day 7

Breakfast
- 1/2 grapefruit
- 1/4 cup Eggbeaters
- *1 Bran Muffin
- 1 cup skim milk

Lunch
- *Italian Tuna Pie
- Vegetable sticks
- Small Apple

Dinner
- *Chicken Teryaki
- 1/2 cup cooked rice
- 1 cup salad
- 2 tab low calorie dressing

Snack
- *Coconut Cooler

Holiday Menu

Brunch

*Puffy Omelet with Strawberries
1/2 cup skim milk

Appetizers

*Oriental Dip (3 tab) with veggies
*Crabmeat Ball with crackers

Dinner

Roast Turkey (3 oz)
*Holiday Carrots
Green Beans
1 cup salad
2 tab low calorie dressing
*Cranberry Corn Muffin
*Pineapple Pie

Snack
*Holiday Nog

APPETIZERS
AND
SNACKS

CRABMEAT BALL

6 oz crabmeat (cooked or canned)
8 oz reduced calorie cream cheese
1/4 cup cocktail sauce

Soften cream cheese and mix thoroughly with crabmeat. Using a fork works best. Shape into a ball and refrigerate.

To serve — spread cocktail sauce over crabmeat ball and serve with crackers.

Serves 12.

Per serving:

Nutrition Information		Exchanges	
cal	67	pro	2/3
pro	4gm	fat	3/4
carb	3gm		
fat	4gm		
satfat	3gm		
chol	18mg		
sod	230mg		

60% of calories from fat
38% of calories from saturated fat

Note: Freezes well.

SARDINE SPREAD

16 oz can sardines, drained
1/4 cup low-sodium catsup
3 tab prepared mustard
1 tsp horseradish
1 tab lemon juice
10 medium salad olives, chopped

Mash sardines with a fork, add rest of ingredients. Mix thoroughly and chill. Serve on crackers, celery or as a sandwich spread.

Serves 16.

Per serving:

Nutrition Information		Exchanges	
cal	58	pro	1/2
pro	5gm	fat	1/2
carb	1gm		
fat	4gm		
satfat	1gm		
chol	17mg		
sod	230mg		

62% of calories from fat
16% of calories from saturated fat

ORIENTAL DIP

1 cup nonfat mayonnaise
1 tab low-sodium soy sauce
1 tsp ginger
1 tsp white vinegar
2 tsp finely chopped onions (optional)

Mix all ingredients together and chill several hours before serving. Serve with cauliflower or other vegetables.

Yield: 1-1/4 cups.

Per serving (1 tab):

Nutrition Information		Exchanges	
cal	11	brd	1/4
pro	0gm		
carb	2gm		
fat	0gm		
satfat	0gm		
chol	0mg		
sod	128mg		

0% of calories from fat
0% of calories from saturated fat

CREAMY TOFU DIP

6 oz tofu
1/2 tsp ginger
2-1/2 tsp low-sodium soy sauce
1 tab tahini or sesame butter
1-1/2 tsp honey

Combine all ingredients in blender and process until smooth. Chill before serving. Serve with vegetables.

Yield: 1-1/4 cups.

Per serving (1 tab):

Nutrition Information		Exchanges
cal	12	none
pro	1gm	
carb	1gm	
fat	1gm	
satfat	0gm	
chol	0mg	
sod	30mg	

75% of calories from fat
0% of calories from saturated fat

HUMMUS

15 oz can garbanzo beans, drain and reserve juice
3 tab tahini or sesame butter
2 tab lemon juice
1/8 tsp garlic powder

Combine all ingredients in blender and process until smooth. If mixture is to thick, add 1 tab at a time of reserved liquid. Mixture should be of dip consistency. Pour into serving dish, sprinkle with paprika and chill. Serve with crackers or pita bread.

Yield: 2 cups, Serves 8.

Per serving (1/4 cup):

Nutrition Information		Exchanges	
cal	89	pro	1/3
pro	4gm	brd	1/2
carb	11gm	fat	3/4
fat	7gm		
satfat	0gm		
chol	0mg		
sod	240mg		

70% of calories from fat
0% of calories from saturated fat

STUFFED ZUCCHINI ROUNDS

2 - 3 zucchini (depending on size)
3 oz reduced calorie cream cheese
1 tab finely chopped green onions with tops
2 tsp chopped parsley
1 tsp nonfat sour cream
1/2 tsp white vinegar

If desired, peel zucchini with potato peeler. Core zucchini to remove the seed section. Set aside to dry. Combine rest of ingredients and stuff zucchini with mixture and chill. Slice and serve chilled.

Yield: 20 slices or rounds.

Per serving (1 slice):

Nutrition Information		Exchanges	
cal	13	fat	1/4
pro	1gm		
carb	0gm		
fat	1gm		
satfat	0gm		
chol	3mg		
sod	1mg		

69% of calories from fat
0% of calories from saturated fat

STUFFED DATES

pitted dates (remove skin if hard)
peanut butter
carob powder

Stuff each pitted date with 1/4 tsp peanut butter. Put carob powder in small sandwich bag, add stuffed dates a few at a time and shake to coat the dates. Store refrigerated.

Per serving (1 date):

Nutrition Information		Exchanges	
cal	31	frt	1/2
pro	1gm		
carb	6gm		
fat	1gm		
satfat	0gm		
chol	0mg		
sod	6mg		

21% of calories from fat
0% of calories from saturated fat

DATE BALLS

pitted dates (remove skin if hard)
unsweetened shredded coconut

Mash dates with a fork until smooth. Put coconut on a flat dish. Shape mashed dates into small balls with hands moistened with water so dates won't stick. Roll dates in coconut to cover. Store in refrigerator. 1 date makes 1 ball.

Per serving (1 ball):

Nutrition Information		Exchanges	
cal	26	frt	1/2
pro	0gm		
carb	6gm		
fat	0gm		
satfat	0gm		
chol	0mg		
sod	1mg		

0% of calories from fat
0% of calories from saturated fat

CITRUS SNACKS

4 envelopes unflavored gelatin
1/4 cup canned unsweetened pineapple juice
1 cup boiling water
4 pkts Equal
1 cup orange juice — no sugar added

In medium bowl, sprinkle gelatin over pineapple juice. Add boiling water and stir until gelatin is completely dissolved. Stir in orange juice and Equal. Pour into 8 or 9 inch square pan and chill until firm. To serve, cut into 1 inch squares.

Makes about 60 1-inch squares.

Note: Must be kept refrigerated.

Serves 10

Per serving (6 pieces):

Nutrition Information		Exchanges	
cal	26	frt	1/4
pro	3gm		
carb	4gm		
fat	0gm		
satfat	0gm		
chol	0mg		
sod	4mg		

0% of calories from fat
0% of calories from saturated fat

GELATIN SNACKS

3 envelopes unflavored gelatin
1 can (12 oz) diet carbonated beverage — heated to boiling
4 pkts Equal
2 tsp extract (see combinations listed below)

In medium bowl, combine gelatin and boiled soda and stir until gelatin is dissolved. Add Equal and extracts and mix well. Pour into 8 X 8 baking pan. Chill until firm. To serve cut into 1 inch squares. Makes about 60 1 inch squares.

Note: Must be kept refrigerated.

Serves 10

Per serving (6 pieces):

Nutrition Information		Exchanges
cal	12	none
pro	2gm	
carb	0gm	
fat	0gm	
satfat	0gm	
chol	0mg	
sod	5mg	

0% of calories from fat
0% of calories from saturated fat

FLAVOR COMBINATIONS

Carbonated Beverage	*Extract*
Cola	Rum
Cream Soda	Vanilla
Black Cherry	Cherry
Lemon/Lime	Lemon
Strawberry	Strawberry
Orange	Orange
Cherry	Cherry

CAROB PEANUT BUTTER CUPS

      8 oz unsweetened carob (block or chips)
      1 tab unsaturated vegetable oil
      1/2 tsp liquid lecithin
      3 tab + 1 tsp peanut butter
      40 1 inch petit-four paper cups

Line a flat tray with the petit-four paper cups. Place carob, oil and liquid lecithin in top of double boiler. Heat until melted, smooth and well blended. Do not over heat.

Using an iced tea spoon, place a small amount of melted carob in petit-four cups. Add 1/4 tsp peanut butter to each candy (this works best using two table knives). Top with additional melted carob. Refrigerate 15 to 20 minutes until firm.

Yield: 40 candies.

Serves 40

Per serving (1 piece):

Nutrition Information		Exchanges	
cal	47	fat	1
pro	1gm		
carb	16gm		
fat	1gm		
satfat	0gm		
chol	0mg		
sod	6mg		

19% of calories from fat
0% of calories from saturated fat

NOTE: To use carob mixture in candy molds, follow instructions for melting the carob, and spoon into molds. Finely chopped raisins, dates or nuts can also be added.

BANANA CHIPS

4 medium bananas, peeled and thinly sliced
1 tsp salt substitute (optional)

Preheat oven to broil. Place banana slices on baking sheets that have been sprayed with release agent. Broil banana slices 30 seconds. Lower oven to 140ºF. Sprinkle banana slices with salt substitute. Dry at 140ºF. (slow oven) for 4 hours, stirring and turning occasionally to prevent sticking.

Serves 4.

Per serving:

Nutrition Information		Exchanges	
cal	105	frt	2
pro	1gm		
carb	27gm		
fat	1gm		
satfat	0gm		
chol	0mg		
sod	1mg		

8% of calories from fat
0% of calories from saturated fat

COCONUT PEANUT BUTTER BALLS

1/3 cup peanut butter
1 tsp vanilla
1 cup unsweetened coconut, grated

In a medium mixing bowl, mix peanut butter and vanilla together, using a fork. Add coconut and mix thoroughly. Shape into balls (approximately 1 tsp each). Dipping your fingers in water occasionally makes the mixture easier to handle. Store in refrigerator.

Yield: 50 pieces.

Per serving (1 ball):

Nutrition Information		Exchanges	
cal	19	fat	1/2
pro	0gm		
carb	1gm		
fat	1gm		
satfat	<1gm		
chol	0mg		
sod	12mg		

47% of calories from fat
33% of calories from saturated fat

VEGGIE DIP

1 cup lowfat cottage cheese
small clove garlic
1 tab chopped chives

Mix all ingredients in blender. Serve chilled and sprinkle with paprika.

Yield: 1 cup. Serves 4 (1/4 cup).

Per serving (1% milkfat):

Nutrition Information		Exchanges	
cal	42	pro	1
pro	7gm		
carb	2gm		
fat	<1gm		
satfat	<1gm		
chol	3mg		
sod	231mg		

11% of calories from fat
9% of calories from saturated fat

Per serving (2% milkfat):

Nutrition Information		Exchanges	
cal	52	pro	1
pro	8gm		
carb	2gm		
fat	1gm		
satfat	<1gm		
chol	5mg		
sod	230mg		

17% of calories from fat
12% of calories from saturated fat

GUACAMOLE

2 ripe avocados, mashed
2 tab lemon juice
1 cup Salsa
2 tab finely chopped parsley (optional)

Sprinkle mashed avocado with the lemon juice and mix. Stir in Salsa and parsley. Garnish as desired.

Yield 2-1/4 cups. Serves 9.

Per serving (1/4 cup):

Nutrition Information		Exchanges	
cal	78	fat	2
pro	1gm		
carb	5gm		
fat	7gm		
satfat	1gm		
chol	0mg		
sod	104mg		

81% of calories from fat
12% of calories from saturated fat

SOUR CREAM (Cottage Cheese)

    1 cup lowfat cottage cheese
    1/4 cup + 1 tab skim milk
    1 tab lemon juice

Place all ingredients in blender and process until smooth. Chill.

Serves 4.

Per Serving (1% milkfat):

Nutrition Information		Exchanges	
cal	47	pro	1
pro	8gm		
carb	3gm		
fat	1gm		
satfat	<1gm		
chol	3mg		
sod	238mg		

12% of calories from fat
8% of calories from saturated fat

Per Serving (2% milkfat):

Nutrition Information		Exchanges	
cal	57	pro	1
pro	8gm		
carb	3gm		
fat	1gm		
satfat	<1gm		
chol	5mg		
sod	238mg		

16% of calories from fat
11% of calories from saturated fat

VEGETABLES
SALADS
AND
DRESSINGS

SPINACH PUFFS

1/2 of 10 oz package frozen chopped spinach, defrosted
1 tab nonfat mayonnaise
1 tab grated Parmesan cheese
1/4 tsp dried onion flakes
1/8 tsp nutmeg
2 egg whites

Place spinach and mayonnaise in mixing bowl. Sprinkle with cheese, onion flakes, and nutmeg. Beat egg whites in a small bowl until soft peaks form. Beat spinach mixture until evenly blended, fold in beaten egg whites. Spoon into 2 8 oz custard cups sprayed with release agent. Bake at 350°F. for 15 - 18 minutes.

MICROWAVE DIRECTIONS. Prepare as above. Microwave on medium power (50%, approximately 325 watts) until set, about 5 minutes.

Serves 2.

Per Serving:

Nutrition Information		Exchanges	
cal	58	pro	3/4
pro	7gm	veg	1
carb	6gm		
fat	1gm		
satfat	<1gm		
chol	2mg		
sod	237mg		

15% of calories from fat
10% of calories from saturated fat

SPINACH PIE

15 oz can whole spinach, well drained
1/2 cup chopped onion
1/4 tsp dried mint leaves, crushed
1/4 tsp allspice
1/4 cup raisins
1 pkg Pillsbury Crescent Rolls (8 count)

Mix all ingredients together except rolls, and set aside. Open rolls and cut each triangle in half. Put spinach mixture in center, fold over and seal edges using fork tines. Bake at 375ºF. 10 to 12 minutes or until lightly browned.

Serves 16.

Per Serving:

Nutrition Information		Exchanges	
cal	65	veg	1/3
pro	2gm	brd	1/2
carb	9gm	fat	1/2
fat	3gm		
satfat	1gm		
chol	3mg		
sod	123mg		

42% of calories from fat
14% of calories from saturated fat

SPINACH PIE

(Continued)

Mini pies for appetizers:

Prepare spinach mixture as above. Using a rolling pin or side of a glass brushed with flour, roll each crescent roll and cut into 3 pieces with a 2-1/2 inch round cookie cutter. Fill and bake as above.

Serves 24.

Per Serving:

Nutrition Information		Exchanges	
cal	43	veg	1/4
pro	1gm	brd	1/4
carb	6gm	fat	1/3
fat	2gm		
satfat	<1gm		
chol	2mg		
sod	90mg		

42% of calories from fat
14% of calories from saturated fat

Note: Freezes well. To re-heat, bake at 350ºF. 8 to 10 minutes.

HOLIDAY CARROTS

1 lb carrots, pared and sliced thin diagonally
1 medium red onion, wedge sliced
12 pitted prunes, cut in quarters
1 tab diet imitation margarine
1/4 cup brown sugar replacement
1/4 tsp ground cinnamon
1/8 tsp nutmeg
1/2 cup orange juice

In a large saucepan combine carrots and onion. Add water just to cover; bring to boil over high heat. Boil rapidly 25 minutes or until carrots are very tender. Drain and put into shallow baking dish. Add prunes.

In a small saucepan, melt margarine, add brown sugar replacement, cinnamon and nutmeg; stir until smooth. Add orange juice. Pour over carrot mixture. Bake 350°F. for 1 hour 20 minutes. Stir every 20 minutes during baking.

MICROWAVE DIRECTIONS. Combine carrots and onion in glass casserole. Add 1/4 cup water. Microwave on high about 10 minutes until carrots are tender. Drain and add prunes.

Mix sauce as above and pour over carrot mixture. Microwave on high another 10 minutes.

Serves 6.

Per Serving:

Nutrition Information		Exchanges	
cal	95	veg	2
pro	2gm	fat	1/4
carb	21gm	frt	3/4
fat	1gm		
satfat	0gm		
chol	0mg		
sod	49mg		

9% of calories from fat
0% of calories from saturated fat

Freezes well.

SPAGHETTI SQUASH CASSEROLE

2-1/2 lb spaghetti squash, washed, cut in half
lengthwise and seeds cleaned out
8 oz tomato sauce — low-sodium
1/8 tsp garlic powder
1 cup grated zucchini
4 oz grated cheddar flavored lowfat cheese
2 tab Parmesan cheese

Prepare squash:

Microwave: Pierce outside and inside of squash with a fork. Place squash with cut side up in baking dish and add 1/4 cup water. Cover with plastic wrap and microwave on high 12 minutes.

Boil: Place cut side down in pan with 2 inches water, cover and boil about 20 minutes.

Run a fork on the inside of the cooked squash to get spaghetti-like strands. Put the strands in a large mixing bowl or casserole.

Mix together tomato sauce and garlic powder. Add zucchini, grated cheese and tomato mixture to spaghetti squash and mix well. Place mixture in casserole or the spaghetti squash shell. Sprinkle Parmesan cheese on top. Bake at 350ºF. for 20 minutes.

Serves 8.

Per Serving:

Nutrition Information		Exchanges	
cal	74	pro	1/2
pro	6gm	veg	1-3/4
carb	9gm		
fat	2gm		
satfat	<1gm		
chol	1mg		
sod	39mg		

24% of calories from fat
5% of calories from saturated fat

Freezes well.

ORANGED SQUASH

16 oz cooked acorn squash, mashed
1/4 tsp cinnamon
1/8 tsp orange extract
sweetener to equal 1/4 cup sugar

Combine all ingredients in saucepan. Cook over low heat about 4 minutes or until heated thoroughly.

MICROWAVE DIRECTIONS. Prepare as above. Microwave on medium power (50%, approximately 325 watts) until heated thoroughly, about 2 minutes.

Serves 4.

Per Serving:

Nutrition Information		Exchanges	
cal	70	brd	1
pro	1gm		
carb	18gm		
fat	0gm		
satfat	0gm		
chol	0mg		
sod	7mg		

0% of calories from fat
0% of calories from saturated fat

ZUCCHINI and ONIONS

3 cups zucchini, thinly sliced
1 cup onion, wedge cuts

Combine all ingredients in sauce pan and simmer about 10 minutes or until vegetables are tender.

Serves 4.

Per Serving:

Nutrition Information		Exchanges	
cal	28	veg	1
pro	2gm		
carb	6gm		
fat	0gm		
satfat	0gm		
chol	0mg		
sod	3mg		

0% of calories from fat
0% of calories from saturated fat

FISH and FRUIT SALAD

1/2 small orange, diced
1 slice pineapple own juice, diced
1 tab pineapple juice
4 oz water pack tuna
1 tab nonfat mayonnaise
2 tsp chopped chives

Toss all ingredients lightly and chill. Serve on lettuce.

Serves 1.

Per Serving:

Nutrition Information		Exchanges	
cal	215	pro	3-1/3
pro	34gm	brd	1/4
carb	17gm	frt	1
fat	<1gm		
satfat	0gm		
chol	0mg		
sod	532mg		

3% of calories from fat
0% of calories from saturated fat

WALDORF SALAD

2 small apples (2-3/4'' diam)
12 large or 20 small grapes
1 cup chopped celery
1/4 cup nonfat mayonnaise
1/4 cup plain nonfat yogurt
2 tab raisins

Combine all ingredients except raisins and chill. Add raisins when ready to serve. Serve on lettuce leaf.

Serves 4.

Per Serving:

Nutrition Information		Exchanges	
cal	77	veg	1/4
pro	1gm	brd	1/4
carb	19gm	frt	1
fat	0gm		
satfat	0gm		
chol	0mg		
sod	38mg		

0% of calories from fat
0% of calories from saturated fat

SOUTHWEST RICE SALAD

3 cups cooked rice (1 cup raw)
3/4 cup nonfat mayonnaise
4 oz reduced calorie cheddar cheese, grated
4 oz can chopped green chiles, drained
1/4 cup chopped pimiento
3/4 cup thinly sliced scallions including green tops

Put chilled cooked rice into a large bowl. Fold in rest of ingredients. Refrigerate several hours before serving. Store refrigerated.

Serves 6.

Per Serving:

Nutrition Information		Exchanges	
cal	179	pro	3/4
pro	7gm	veg	1/3
carb	33gm	brd	2
fat	1gm		
satfat	0gm		
chol	0mg		
sod	329mg		

5% of calories from fat
0% of calories from saturated fat

CHICKEN SALAD

3 oz cooked chicken breast, diced
1/3 cup chopped celery
1/4 cup sliced fresh mushrooms
1 tab nonfat mayonnaise

Mix all ingredients together and chill.

Serves 1.

Per Serving:

Nutrition Information		Exchanges	
cal	162	pro	3
pro	27gm	veg	1/2
carb	5gm	brd	1/4
fat	3gm		
satfat	1gm		
chol	72mg		
sod	219mg		

17% of calories from fat
5% of calories from saturated fat

SWEET and SOUR COLE SLAW

1/3 cup white vinegar
3 tab vegetable oil
1 tab brown sugar replacement
1 tsp dehydrated onion flakes
1/2 tsp dry mustard
1/4 tsp pepper (optional)
2 tab chopped pimientos
4 cups shredded cabbage

Combine all ingredients except pimentos and cabbage in a large bowl. Add pimientos and cabbage, toss well. Cover and chill before serving. Store refrigerated.

Serves 9.

Per Serving:

Nutrition Information		Exchanges	
cal	53	veg	1/2
pro	1gm	fat	1
carb	3gm		
fat	5gm		
satfat	<1gm		
chol	0mg		
sod	15mg		

85% of calories from fat
7% of calories from saturated fat

TUNA SALAD

3 oz water-pack tuna, low-sodium
1/3 cup chopped celery
1 tab chopped onion
1 tab nonfat mayonnaise

Mix all ingredients together and chill.

Serves 1.

Per Serving:

Nutrition Information		Exchanges	
cal	125	pro	2-1/2
pro	23gm	veg	1/2
carb	4gm	brd	1/4
fat	<2gm		
satfat	0gm		
chol	30mg		
sod	191mg		

12% of calories from fat
0% of calories from saturated fat

CUCUMBER SALAD DRESSING

1/2 cup cucumber
1/2 cup nonfat mayonnaise
1 tab minced onion or chives

If creamy texture is desired, pare cucumber. Unpared cucumber results in a chunkier dressing with flecks of dark green.

Shred or finely chop the cucumber. Combine all ingredients in blender and blend until smooth. Store in covered container in refrigerator.

Yield: 1 cup.

Per Serving (1 tab):

Nutrition Information		Exchanges
cal	7	none
pro	0gm	
carb	1gm	
fat	0gm	
satfat	0gm	
chol	3mg	
sod	62mg	

0% of calories from fat
0% of calories from saturated fat

CRANBERRY CHUTNEY

1 16 oz can whole cranberry sauce
1/2 cup raisins
1/2 cup chopped peach or pineapple
1/2 tsp ground ginger

Mix all ingredients together and chill overnight before serving.

Yield: 3 cups. Serves 12.

Per Serving (1/4 cup):

Nutrition Information		Exchanges	
cal	95	frt	1-1/2
pro	0gm		
carb	25gm		
fat	0gm		
satfat	0gm		
chol	0mg		
sod	15mg		

0% of calories from fat
0% of calories from saturated fat

FRENCH DRESSING

1/2 cup tomato juice — low-sodium
1/4 cup cider or wine vinegar
1 tab finely chopped onion
pepper to taste (optional)

Mix all ingredients and put into jar. Shake well before serving. Store refrigerated.

Yield: 3/4 cup.

Per Serving (1 tab):

Nutrition Information		Exchanges	
cal	2	veg	1/8
pro	0gm		
carb	1gm		
fat	0gm		
satfat	0gm		
chol	0mg		
sod	1mg		

0% of calories from fat
0% of calories from saturated fat

HONEY-MUSTARD DRESSING

1 tab honey
1 tab Dijon-style mustard
1/8 tsp pepper
8 oz plain nonfat yogurt

In a small bowl, mix together (with a spoon or wire whisk) honey, mustard and pepper until well blended. Stir in yogurt gently with spoon and mix well.

Yield: 1 cup.

Per Serving (1 tab):

Nutrition Information		Exchanges
cal	13	none
pro	1gm	
carb	2gm	
fat	0gm	
satfat	0gm	
chol	0mg	
sod	23mg	

0% of calories from fat
0% of calories from saturated fat

TERIYAKI MARINADE

1/4 cup low-sodium soy sauce
1/4 cup white vinegar
1 tsp ginger
Sugar sub to equal 4 tsp sugar (2 pkts)
1/2 tsp garlic powder

Mix all ingredients well and put in jar. Stir well before serving. Store refrigerated. Use for chicken or fish.

Yield: 1/2 cup.

Per 1/2 cup:

Nutrition Information

Exchanges

cal	78	none
pro	6gm	
carb	15gm	
fat	0gm	
satfat	0gm	
chol	0mg	
sod	2266mg	

0% of calories from fat
0% of calories from saturated fat

ENTREES

CHICKEN KABOBS

2 cups pineapple chunks, own juice no sugar added
16 oz chicken breast, skinned and boned
2 tab low calorie Italian salad dressing (6 calories per tab)
1 tab Worcestershire sauce
1/4 tsp cinnamon

Drain pineapple and reserve the juice. Cut chicken into 1 inch cubes. Place on skewers, alternating with the pineapple chunks. Brush evenly with the Italian salad dressing and allow to marinate at least one hour (overnight is good also).

Preheat broiler or BBQ. Broil or BBQ about 15 minutes or until cooked and lightly browned, turning after 8 minutes. While kabobs are cooking, combine pineapple juice, Worcestershire sauce and cinnamon in a small saucepan. Simmer about 10 minutes. Spoon over kabobs before serving.

Serves 4.

Per Serving:

Nutrition Information		Exchanges	
cal	222	pro	3
pro	26gm	fat	1/3
carb	19gm	frt	1
fat	7gm		
satfat	2gm		
chol	72mg		
sod	136mg		

28% of calories from fat
8% of calories from saturated fat

NOTE: This works well with turkey also. Great served with rice (not included in nutrition information).

CHICKEN TERIYAKI

2 lbs chicken or parts
1/2 cup Teriyaki Marinade (see index)
20 oz can pineapple chunks, own juice no sugar added
16 oz package frozen mixed or fresh vegetables (broccoli, mushrooms)

Cut chicken into parts if whole. Wash, remove skin and all visible fat. Arrange chicken pieces in 10 inch skillet or pan that has a cover. Chicken should be in one layer only. Pierce chicken pieces with a fork. Pour Teriyaki sauce evenly over chicken. Arrange pineapple chunks (and fresh vegetables if used) on top of chicken. Add pineapple juice. Cover and refrigerate overnight to marinate (up to 24 hours).

When ready to cook, add package of frozen vegetables (if used) on top of pineapple and chicken. Cover and simmer slow on top of stove approximately 45 minutes or until done.

Serves 5.

Per Serving:

Nutrition Information		Exchanges	
cal	291	pro	4
pro	38gm	veg	1
carb	24gm	frt	1
fat	4gm		
satfat	1gm		
chol	96mg		
sod	553mg		

12% of calories from fat
4% of calories from saturated fat

NOTE: This is a great make-ahead meal. Serve with rice (nutrition information not included).

CHICKEN DIJON

2 4 oz chicken breasts, boned and skinless
1/4 cup dry white wine
1/4 tsp dried tarragon
1 tsp Dijon mustard

In a medium skillet that has been sprayed with a release agent and heated, cook chicken breasts on medium heat about 3 minutes, turn and cook additional 2 minutes. Remove chicken breasts from skillet and set aside. Add white wine, tarragon and Dijon mustard to skillet and cook on high heat until syrupy (about 2 minutes). Add chicken breasts and heat slightly. Serve with the syrup poured over the chicken.

Serves 2.

Per Serving:

Nutrition Information

		Exchanges	
cal	163	pro	3
pro	27gm	fat	1/8
carb	0gm		
fat	3gm		
satfat	<1gm		
chol	72mg		
sod	115mg		

17% of calories from fat
1% of calories from saturated fat

CRABMEAT MELT

2 oz crabmeat
1/2 cup (2 oz) shredded lowfat cheese, divided
1/4 cup chopped green bell pepper
2 tab nonfat mayonnaise
4 tab imitation sour cream
1 English muffin, split and toasted
2 fresh mushrooms sliced
2 tsp Baco's (imitation Bacon bits, made with soybean)

Combine crabmeat, 1/4 cup cheese, green pepper, mayonnaise and sour cream. Mix well. Divide evenly and place on toasted muffin halves. Add mushrooms, sprinkle with remaining cheese and top with Baco's. Broil 3 to 5 minutes or until cheese is melted.

Serves 2.

Per Serving:

Nutrition Information		Exchanges	
cal	223	pro	1-3/4
pro	15gm	veg	1/4
carb	23gm	brd	1
fat	8gm	fat	1-1/2
satfat	4gm		
chol	6mg		
sod	628mg		

32% of calories from fat
16% of calories from saturated fat

EGG ROLLS

        12 oz cooked chicken breast, chopped
        1 tab cornstarch
        1 tab unsaturated vegetable oil
        2 cups bean sprouts, chopped
        1/2 cup green onions, chopped fine
        1/2 cup mushrooms, chopped fine
        3/4 cup cooked spinach, chopped
        2 tab low-sodium soy sauce
        3/4 cup Eggbeaters

Mix together chicken and cornstarch, and set aside.

Saute using 1 tab oil; bean sprouts and green onion about 2 minutes. Add mushrooms and spinach, saute 1 minute. Add soy sauce and remove from heat. Add chicken mixture.

WRAPPERS

Beat 1/4 cup Eggbeaters with 1 tab water. Pour half into frying pan sprayed with release agent. Cook on both sides. Place 1/6 of filling on Eggbeater and roll. Place in baking dish sprayed with release agent, with seam side down. Repeat for remainder of rolls. Bake 350°F. about 15 minutes.

Serves 6.

                        Per Serving:
        Nutrition Information   Exchanges

        cal   156   pro   2-1/2
        pro   23gm   veg   1
        carb   6gm   fat   1/2
        fat   4gm
        satfat   1gm
        chol   48mg
        sod   294mg

23% of calories from fat
5% of calories from saturated fat

EGGPLANT ITALIAN STYLE

1 lb ground turkey
1 cup chopped onion
1/4 tsp garlic powder
1/2 tsp pepper (optional)
2 cups water
3 sodium free chicken bullion cubes
2 medium eggplant
1 8 oz can chopped tomato
1 8 oz can tomato sauce
1/2 tsp oregano

Saute ground turkey and onion. Add garlic powder and pepper, set aside.

In a large skillet or pan, bring 2 cups water to boil and add the chicken bullion cubes. Wash eggplant and remove top. Cut into 1/2 inch thick slices, leaving skin on. Simmer about 5 minutes or until fork can be inserted. Eggplant will still be firm.

Place eggplant slices in baking pans that have been sprayed with release agent. Spoon meat mixture on each slice. Mix chopped tomatoes, tomato sauce and oregano together with remainder of chicken broth. Spoon evenly over meat covered eggplant slices. Bake 350ºF. about 45 to 50 minutes. Serve with rice.

Serves 6.

Per Serving:

Nutrition Information		Exchanges	
cal	210	pro	2
pro	15gm	veg	2-1/2
carb	15gm	fat	3/4
fat	12gm		
satfat	2gm		
chol	0mg		
sod	135mg		

51% of calories from fat
10% of calories from saturated fat

Freezes well. Rice not included in nutrition information.

EGGPLANT MID-EAST STYLE

        1 lb ground turkey
        1 cup chopped onion
        1/2 tsp allspice
        1/4 tsp cinnamon
        1/4 tsp garlic powder, divided
        2 medium eggplant
        2 cups water
        1 8 oz can tomato sauce
        1/2 tsp dried mint leaves, crushed

Saute ground turkey and onion with allspice, cinnamon, 1/8 tsp garlic powder and set aside.

Wash eggplant and remove tops. Cut into 1/2 inch slices, leaving skin on. Broil eggplant slices 5 to 10 minutes on each side or until browned. Eggplant will still be slightly firm.

Place eggplant slices in baking pans that have been sprayed with release agent. Spoon meat mixture on each slice.

Make sauce by combining water, tomato sauce, dried mint and remaining garlic powder. Simmer 5 minutes. Spoon evenly over meat covered eggplant slices. Bake 400ºF. 30 minutes. Serve with rice.

Serves 6.

Per Serving:

Nutrition Information		Exchanges	
cal	200	pro	2
pro	14gm	veg	2-1/3
carb	12gm	fat	3/4
fat	11gm		
satfat	2gm		
chol	0mg		
sod	74mg		

50% of calories from fat
10% of calories from saturated fat

Freezes well. Rice not included in nutrition information.

ORANGE GLAZED FISH

9 oz halibut steaks (or cod)
1 tab green onion, chopped
2 tsp diet imitation margarine
2 tsp cornstarch
1/2 cup orange juice
1/2 tsp sodium free chicken broth granules
1/2 small orange, peeled, sectioned and diced

Arrange fish in shallow baking dish. In a small saucepan, cook the green onion in margarine until tender. Add the cornstarch and blend well. Add orange juice and chicken broth granules. Cook until thickened and bubbly, stirring constantly. Remove from heat and add diced orange. Pour over fish.

Bake 350ºF. about 20 minutes or until fish flakes.

Serves 2.

Per Serving:

Nutrition Information		Exchanges	
cal	210	pro	3
pro	28gm	brd	1/4
carb	15gm	fat	1/4
fat	4gm	frt	1
satfat	<1gm		
chol	41mg		
sod	91mg		

17% of calories from fat
3% of calories from saturated fat

POACHED FISH

1 lb fish filets, fresh or frozen
1 tab lemon juice

Place fish filets in skillet and cover with boiling water. Add lemon juice.

Cover and simmer until fish flakes when tested with a fork. This takes only a few minutes depending on thickness of filets (1/2 inch thick filets — 5 minutes) and whether fish is fresh or frozen.

Serves 4.

Per Serving:

Nutrition Information		Exchanges	
cal	114	pro	2-1/2
pro	23gm		
carb	0gm		
fat	<2gm		
satfat	<1gm		
chol	41mg		
sod	73mg		

12% of calories from fat
3% of calories from saturated fat

TERIYAKI FISH

1 lb fish filets
1/4 cup Teriyaki Marinade (see index)

Marinate fish filets in Teryaki sauce 15 minutes. Bake 400ºF. 20 minutes or until fish flakes.

Serves 4.

Per Serving:

Nutrition Information		Exchanges	
cal	123	pro	2-1/2
pro	24gm		
carb	2gm		
fat	<2gm		
satfat	<1gm		
chol	41mg		
sod	366mg		

11% of calories from fat
3% of calories from saturated fat

POLYNESIAN FISH

1 cup pineapple chunks, own juice no sugar added,
    drained
1/2 medium green pepper, chopped
1 medium tomato, chopped
1 tab white vinegar
2 tsp low-sodium soy sauce
1/2 tsp ground ginger
8 oz fish cut into bite size pieces

Combine pineapple, green pepper, tomato, vinegar, soy sauce and ginger in saucepan. Cook over medium heat 10 to 15 minutes stirring occasionally. Place fish on top of sauce, cover and cook 10 minutes or until fish is done.

Serves 2.

Per Serving:

Nutrition Information		Exchanges	
cal	207	pro	2-1/2
pro	24gm	veg	3/4
carb	23gm	frt	1
fat	<2gm		
satfat	<1gm		
chol	41mg		
sod	276mg		

7% of calories from fat
2% of calories from saturated fat

STUFFED GRAPE LEAVES

1 quart grape leaves (approx. 80), rinse thoroughly and
place in colander to drain

Stuffing:

3/4 cup long grain rice, uncooked and rinsed in cold water
1-1/2 lbs ground turkey
1/4 tsp cinnamon
2 tsp allspice
1/2 tsp pepper (optional)

Combine all ingredients for stuffing and mix together loosely —
do not pack down.

Place one grape leaf on a plate, vein side up, and put a small
amount of stuffing (about the size of your small finger) at the widest
part (base) of the leaf. Fold in both sides of leaf and roll up.

Place leftover or broken leaves on wire rack in bottom of deep
pan. Arrange stuffed grape leaves side by side and in layers. Place
a heat resistant plate on top of the grape leaves to keep them
from floating and unrolling during cooking. Put a weight (a jar
filled with water) on the plate. Partially cover grape leaves with
boiling water. If desired, a little lemon juice can be added for
flavoring. Simmer approximately 45 minutes or until done. Serve
with lemon juice or yogurt.

Serves 16.

Per Serving (5 pieces):

Nutrition Information		Exchanges	
cal	251	pro	1-1/4
pro	9gm	brd	2-1/2
carb	40gm	fat	1/3
fat	6gm		
satfat	<2gm		
chol	0mg		
sod	144mg		

22% of calories from fat
5% of calories from saturated fat

Freezes well.

GARBANZO BURGERS

12 oz can garbanzo beans, drained
(also called chickpeas)
2 oz onion, chopped
2 tab chopped fresh parsley
2 tsp lemon juice
1/2 tsp basil
1/4 tsp oregano
Dash cumin and garlic powder

Grind garbanzos with a meat grinder. In a non-stick skillet, cook onion until soft. Place all ingredients in a mixing bowl and mix thoroughly with a fork. Shape into 2 equal patties; place on non-stick baking sheet or one sprayed with release agent. Bake at 350ºF. 30 minutes, turning once, until firm.

Serves 2.

Per Serving:

Nutrition Information		Exchanges	
cal	180	pro	1
pro	8gm	veg	1/2
carb	31gm	brd	1-3/4
fat	3gm		
satfat	0gm		
chol	0mg		
sod	679mg		

15% of calories from fat
0% of calories from saturated fat

ITALIAN TUNA PIE

1 can (6-1/2 oz) water-pack tuna, drained and flaked
1/2 cup chopped onion
1 cup chopped fresh tomato
12 black olives, sliced
1/2 cup chopped green pepper
3 egg whites
1/4 cup Eggbeaters
1-1/4 cups skim milk
3/4 cup Basic Baking Mix (see index)
1 tsp oregano crushed
1/4 tsp garlic powder

Spread tuna evenly in bottom of 10 inch pie plate that has been sprayed with release agent. Add in layers — onion, tomato, olives and green pepper. With electric mixer, beat egg whites, Eggbeaters and milk together, add basic baking mix, oregano and garlic powder. Beat until smooth (about 1 minute). Pour mixture over tuna. Bake at 400ºF. 25 to 30 minutes, or until a knife inserted in center comes out clean. Allow to stand 5 minutes before cutting.

Serves 6.

Per Serving:

Nutrition Information		Exchanges	
cal	152	pro	1-1/3
pro	15gm	veg	1/2
carb	15gm	brd	2/3
fat	<4gm	fat	3/4
satfat	<1gm	milk	1/4
chol	1mg		
sod	308mg		

22% of calories from fat
4% of calories from saturated fat

BAKED KIBBEE

2 cups Bulgur (fine grind)
2/3 tsp marjoram
1-1/2 tsp allspice
1/2 tsp pepper (optional)
2 lbs ground turkey
Paprika

Soak bulgur in water (just cover, about 1-1/2 cups water) approximately 20 minutes until water is absorbed. Toss lightly with fork; add seasonings mixing thoroughly. In a large bowl mix ground turkey, and seasoned bulgur, kneading well with hands. If mixture is dry, add a little water. Knead for about 10 minutes to insure a good mixture.

Spread mixture evenly in a 9 X 13 X 2 pan that has been sprayed with release agent. Score top of meat with a diamond design. Sprinkle with paprika.

Bake 400ºF. about 20 minutes.

Serves 10.

Per Serving:

Nutrition Information		Exchanges	
cal	302	pro	2-1/2
pro	17gm	brd	1-3/4
carb	28gm	fat	1
fat	13gm		
satfat	0gm		
chol	0mg		
sod	72mg		

39% of calories from fat
0% of calories from saturated fat

Freezes well.

BAKED STUFFED KIBBEE

Stuffing:

>   1 lb ground turkey
>   2 cups chopped onion
>   1 tsp allspice

Combine all ingredients in large skillet sprayed with release agent and saute until onion transparent and meat just cooked (do not over cook). Remove from heat and set aside.

Kibbee:

>   2 cups Bulgur (fine grind)
>   1 tsp ground marjoram
>   2 tsp allspice
>   1/2 tsp pepper (optional)
>   3 lbs ground turkey
>   Pine nuts (optional)
>   Paprika

Soak bulgur in water (just cover, about 1-1/2 cups water) approximately 20 minutes until water is absorbed. Toss lightly with fork; add seasonings and mix thoroughly. In a large bowl mix ground turkey, and seasoned bulgur, kneading well with hands. If mixture is dry, add a little water. Knead for about 10 minutes to insure a good mixture.

Measure mixture into slight 2 oz balls. Roll each ball in hands and make a hole in center to add stuffing (about 1/4 of ball is stuffing). Close meat around stuffing and shape like a football. Place on baking trays sprayed with release agent. Sprinkle with paprika.

Optional: Add 3 pine nuts to each ball when stuffing.

Bake 400ºF. about 20 minutes.

Yield 38 pieces.

BAKED STUFFED KIBBEE
(Continued)

Per Serving (1 piece):

Nutrition Information		Exchanges	
cal	128	pro	1-1/3
pro	8gm	brd	1/2
carb	8gm	fat	1/2
fat	7gm		
satfat	0gm		
chol	0mg		
sod	38mg		

49% of calories from fat
0% of calories from saturated fat

Freezes well.

LASAGNA FLORENTINE

1 10 oz pkg frozen chopped spinach, thawed and drained
1 tab unsaturated vegetable oil
1 cup finely chopped onion
2 cloves garlic, crushed
3/4 tsp basil
1/2 tsp oregano
1/2 bay leaf
1 can (2 lb 3 oz) Italian tomatoes, mashed
1 can (8 oz) tomato sauce
2 tab chopped parsley
9 lasagna noodles (1/2 of 1 lb pkg)
2 cups (16 oz) lowfat cottage cheese (1% milkfat)
3 tab grated Parmesan cheese

Drain spinach well on paper towels. In a 5 quart pan, saute onion, garlic, basil, oregano and bay leaf in the oil, stirring for about 2 minutes. Add mashed tomatoes, tomato sauce and parsley, mixing well. Bring to boil, reduce heat, simmer about 10 minutes. Makes 4 cups sauce.

Preheat oven to 375°F. Cook lasagna according to package directions and drain well.

Using a 2 quart shallow baking dish sprayed with release agent, spoon 1 cup of sauce in bottom of baking dish. Layer with three (3) lasagna noodles, over-lapping to cover. Spread 1/2 of the spinach, 1 cup cottage cheese and 1 cup of sauce over the lasagna layer.

Make another layer and top with remaining lasagna noodles. Spread remaining sauce on top. Sprinkle with Parmesan cheese.

Cover with aluminum foil, tucking around edges. Bake 25 minutes; remove foil, and bake uncovered additional 25 minutes or until bubbly. Let stand 10 minutes before serving.

LASAGNA FLORENTINE
(continued)

Serves 8.

Per Serving:

Nutrition Information		Exchanges	
cal	155	pro	1
pro	12gm	veg	2
carb	19gm	brd	1/2
fat	<4gm	fat	1/2
satfat	1gm		
chol	13mg		
sod	508mg		

21% of calories from fat
6% of calories from saturated fat

TOFU STIR FRY

1 tab unsaturated vegetable oil
3/4 cup celery pieces
3/4 cup bean sprouts
1/4 cup onion, wedge sliced
4 oz tofu, cut in small pieces

Place oil in non-stick frying pan and heat. Add vegetables and cook until sprouts and onions transparent, stirring occasionally. Add tofu and cook 1 more minute. Serve immediately. Optional — sprinkle with low-sodium soy sauce.

Serves 1.

Per Serving:

Nutrition Information		Exchanges	
cal	336	pro	2-1/2
pro	21gm	veg	2-1/4
carb	16gm	fat	3-1/4
fat	24gm		
satfat	3gm		
chol	0mg		
sod	100mg		

64% of calories from fat
9% of calories from saturated fat

MEXICAN BEAN CASSEROLE

        1/2 cup chopped onion
        1 clove garlic, minced or 1/8 tsp garlic powder
        16 oz can tomatoes, cut up
        15-1/2 oz can red kidney beans, drained and rinsed
        15 oz can garbanzo beans, drained and rinsed
        4 oz can chopped green chili peppers, drained
        1 tsp chili pepper (optional)
        2 tab cold water
        1 tab all purpose flour
        2 cups water
        3/4 cup yellow corn meal

Cook onion and garlic in large saucepan until tender. Stir in tomatoes, kidney and garbanzo beans, green chili peppers and chili powder. Bring to boil and reduce heat. Stir together 2 tab water and flour, add to mixture. Cook and stir until thick and bubbly. Keep warm while preparing the following.

In a medium saucepan, combine 2 cups water and cornmeal. Cook and stir until thick and bubbly.

Spoon hot bean mixture into a 12 X 7-1/2 X 2 baking dish that has been sprayed with release agent. Spoon cornmeal mixture over the bean mixture. Bake at 375ºF. 25 minutes or until cornmeal is light brown.

Serves 10.

                        Per Serving:
        Nutrition Information   Exchanges

        cal   126   pro   1/4
        pro   6gm   veg   2/3
        carb   24gm   brd   1-1/2
        fat   1gm
        satfat   1gm
        chol   0mg
        sod   251mg

7% of calories from fat
7% of calories from saturated fat

MEXICAN STYLE MEATLOAF

1-1/2 pounds ground turkey
1 can (16 oz) low-sodium red kidney beans, rinsed
      and drained
2/3 cup salsa
3/4 cup chopped onion
1/4 tsp garlic powder or 1 clove garlic
1/2 cup bread crumbs
2 egg whites, lightly beaten
2 tab brown sugar substitute

Mix all ingredients together and mix thoroughly. Put mixture into a 9 x 5 loaf pan that has been sprayed with release agent. Press mixture to remove air pockets. Bake at 350^{0}F 1 hour. Let stand 10 minutes before serving. If using glass baking pan, bake at 325^{0}F.

Serves 8.

Per Serving:

Nutrition Information		Exchanges	
cal	252	pro	2-1/2
pro	19gm	veg	1/4
carb	15gm	brd	1
fat	13gm	fat	3/4
satfat	0gm		
chol	0mg		
sod	203mg		

46% of calories from fat
0% of calories from saturated fat

Freezes well.

SALMON ROAST BBQ

Thaw salmon roast before cooking, approximately 30 minutes in cool water or several hours in refrigerator. The center bone will remove easily after cooking.

Mix together:

> 1/4 cup diet imitation margarine melted or
> Butter Buds
> 1 tsp lemon juice
> 1/4 tsp garlic powder

Split thawed salmon in half lengthwise along the center bone. Place salmon halves, skin side down, on grill or in foil lined pan on grill. Baste with the lemon butter mixture and cook with the grill cover closed 20 to 30 minutes until done (depending on thickness of salmon).

Serves 4.

Per Serving (3 oz):

Nutrition Information		Exchanges	
cal	208	pro	3
pro	23gm	fat	1
carb	0gm		
fat	12gm		
satfat	2gm		
chol	42mg		
sod	180mg		

52% of calories from fat
9% of calories from saturated fat

NOTE: Can also be baked in 375°F. oven 20 to 30 minutes per pound.

SCALLOPED TUNA

1 10 oz pkg frozen French-cut green beans, cooked
     and drained
2 6-1/2 oz cans water-pack tuna, drained
4 oz can mushrooms stem and pieces, drained
1/2 cup chopped celery
1 tsp instant minced onion
1 tsp garlic powder
1/2 tsp dill weed
1 cup evaporated skim milk

In bowl combine all ingredients and mix well. Pour into 1-1/2 quart
baking dish that has been sprayed with release agent. Bake at
350ºF. for 30 minutes.

Serves 4.

Per Serving:

Nutrition Information		Exchanges	
cal	187	pro	2-1/2
pro	30gm	veg	1
carb	14gm	milk	2/3
fat	2gm		
satfat	0gm		
chol	32mg		
sod	130mg		

10% of calories from fat
0% of calories from saturated fat

SPICY TUNA CASSEROLE

3 egg whites
1/4 cup Eggbeaters
1 6-1/2 oz can water-pack tuna, drained
1 4 oz can diced green chili peppers
1 cup finely chopped onion
1 tab chopped parsley
4 tab grated Parmesan cheese

Beat egg whites and Eggbeaters together. Combine all ingredients except grated cheese and mix well. Place in baking dish sprayed with release agent.

Bake 400°F. 45 minutes.

Sprinkle grated cheese on top before serving.

Serves 4.

Per Serving:

Nutrition Information		Exchanges	
cal	126	pro	2-1/2
pro	19gm	veg	3/4
carb	5gm		
fat	3gm		
satfat	1gm		
chol	21mg		
sod	198mg		

21% of calories from fat
9% of calories from saturated fat

TUNA LOAF

2 egg whites
1/4 cup Eggbeaters
4 oz water-pack tuna, drained
2 slices white bread, crumbed
2 tab diet imitation margarine
1 tab parsley flakes
1 tab pimiento, chopped
1/8 tsp seasoning (optional)

Beat egg whites and Eggbeaters together. In a bowl combine all ingredients and mix well. Spoon into non-stick baking dish. Set baking dish in pan of hot water.

Bake at 350ºF. 30 minutes or until firm. Serve hot or cold. Garnish with cucumber slices or cold sliced vegetables.

Serves 2.

Per Serving:

Nutrition Information		Exchanges	
cal	227	pro	2-3/4
pro	24gm	brd	3/4
carb	14gm	fat	1-1/3
fat	8gm		
satfat	1gm		
chol	20mg		
sod	378mg		

32% of calories from fat
5% of calories from saturated fat

TUNA MUSHROOM DIABLO

6 oz water-pack tuna, drained
2 cups sliced fresh mushrooms
8 oz pkg frozen peas
1/2 cup sliced celery
2 tab skim milk
1/2 tsp dry mustard
2 tab nonfat mayonnaise
1 tab chopped pimiento, drained
1 tsp white wine vinegar
2 slices whole wheat bread, toasted

In a skillet combine tuna, mushrooms, peas, celery, skim milk and dry mustard. Bring to a boil, cover and simmer 5 minutes over medium heat. Combine mayonnaise, pimiento and vinegar. Stir into tuna mixture.

Serve with toast.

Serves 2.

Per Serving:

Nutrition Information		Exchanges	
cal	282	pro	2-1/2
pro	32gm	veg	1
carb	33gm	brd	1-3/4
fat	3gm	fat	1-1/4
satfat	0gm		
chol	34mg		
sod	440mg		

11% of calories from fat
0% of calories from saturated fat

TUNA STUFFED PEPPERS

4 large green peppers
4 tab dry bread crumbs
3 tab tarragon vinegar
1/4 tsp garlic powder
12 oz water-pack tuna low-sodium, drained
4 tab nonfat mayonnaise
2 tab water

Cut peppers in half and remove membrane and seeds. Combine the bread crumbs, vinegar, garlic powder, tuna and mayonnaise.

Stuff the green peppers and place in a shallow pan, adding the 2 tab water.

Bake at 350⁰F. 45 to 50 minutes.

Serves 4.

Per Serving:

Nutrition Information		Exchanges	
cal	162	pro	2-1/2
pro	24gm	veg	3/4
carb	12gm	brd	1/2
fat	2gm		
satfat	0gm		
chol	30mg		
sod	207mg		

11% of calories from fat
0% of calories from saturated fat

TURKEY BURGERS

1 lb ground turkey
1/3 cup finely chopped onions
1/2 cup Italian seasoned bread crumbs
1/2 tsp garlic powder
1 tsp Worcestershire sauce
1/2 tsp prepared mustard
1/4 cup Eggbeaters

In a large bowl, combine all ingredients and mix well. Shape into 5 patties about 1/2 inch thick (patties will puff up when cooked). Broil on broiling pan or grill that has been sprayed with release agent 4 to 5 minutes each side, or until done in center (not pink). Serve as is or on buns.

Serves 5.

Per Serving:

Nutrition Information		Exchanges	
cal	225	pro	2-3/4
pro	17gm	brd	1/2
carb	9gm	fat	1
fat	13gm		
satfat	0gm		
chol	0mg		
sod	178mg		

52% of calories from fat
0% of calories from saturated fat

Note: Freezes well.
Bun not included in nutritional information.

TURKEY DIVAN

10 oz pkg frozen broccoli spears
8 oz cooked turkey breast, thickly sliced
2 pkg low-sodium mushroom soup mix
1/2 cup skim milk
1/3 cup lowfat cheddar cheese, shredded

Cook broccoli according to package directions, drain. Arrange broccoli in a 1-1/2 quart casserole or 9 inch round baking dish, with stems towards the middle. Place turkey slices evenly on top.

Combine soup mix with 1/2 cup boiling water. Blend in the milk and cheese. Pour sauce over the turkey.

Bake 375ºF. 25 minutes or until sauce begins to bubble.

Serves 4.

Per Serving:

Nutrition Information		Exchanges	
cal	164	pro	2
pro	24gm	veg	3/4
carb	8gm	brd	1/4
fat	<4gm	fat	1
satfat	<1gm		
chol	58mg		
sod	319mg		

20% of calories from fat
4% of calories from saturated fat

TURKEY LOAF I

1 lb ground turkey
1/2 cup Millers bran
1/3 to 1/2 cup low-sodium tomato juice
2 egg whites or 1/4 cup Eggbeaters
3 tab chopped onion
1 tsp allspice
1 tsp Worcestershire sauce

Mix all ingredients well and place in loaf pan sprayed with release agent. Bake 350ºF. 1 hour.

Serves 5.

Per Serving:

Nutrition Information		Exchanges	
cal	214	pro	2-3/4
pro	18gm	veg	1/4
carb	6gm	brd	1/3
fat	13gm	fat	1
satfat	3gm		
chol	0mg		
sod	107mg		

55% of calories from fat
13% of calories from saturated fat

Freezes well.

TURKEY LOAF II

2-1/2 lbs ground turkey
1 cup Millers bran
1/3 cup lite catsup
2 egg whites or 1/4 cup Eggbeaters
2-1/2 tsp allspice
1 tsp marjoram
1/8 tsp garlic powder

Mix all ingredients well and place in loaf pan sprayed with release agent. Bake 350ºF. 1 hour.

Serves 8.

Per Serving:

Nutrition Information		Exchanges	
cal	254	pro	3-1/4
pro	20gm	brd	1/3
carb	5gm	fat	1
fat	16gm		
satfat	<4gm		
chol	0mg		
sod	132mg		

57% of calories from fat
13% of calories from saturated fat

Freezes well.

STUFFED ZUCCHINI

1 dozen zucchini squash
1/4 tsp garlic powder
1 tab dried mint, crushed
1 can (20 oz) solid pack low-sodium tomatoes cut in pieces
    (optional)

1 recipe stuffing (see Stuffed Grape Leaves)

Wash outside of squash, cut off top and core, leaving a thin shell. Scrape off the root end. Rinse squash in a bowl of cold water containing the garlic and mint.

Stuff squash loosely.

Place squash on a wire rack in deep pan, add cut tomatoes and garlic/mint water to cover squash. Cover and cook on slow simmer approximately 35 minutes or until tender.

Serves 6.

Per Serving:

Nutrition Information		Exchanges	
cal	352	pro	3
pro	22gm	veg	2
carb	30gm	brd	1-1/4
fat	16gm	fat	1
satfat	3gm		
chol	0mg		
sod	107mg		

41% of calories from fat
9% of calories from saturated fat

Freezes well. Freeze sauce separate from squash.

Notes:

DESSERTS

MOUSSE

1/4 cup cold water
1 envelope unflavored gelatin
1/4 cup boiling water
1 pkt Alba 77
1 pkt sweetener (optional)
4 - 6 ice cubes crushed

Place cold water in blender. Add unflavored gelatin. Blend on low 10 seconds. Add boiling water and blend on high 10 seconds. Add Alba and sweetener, blend another 10 seconds. Add crushed ice cubes one at a time while blending on high. Pour into dish and serve.

Do not make too far ahead as it will break down.

Serves 1.

Per Serving:

Nutrition Information		Exchanges	
cal	99	milk	1
pro	11gm		
carb	12gm		
fat	0gm		
satfat	0gm		
chol	0mg		
sod	162mg		

0% of calories from fat
0% of calories from saturated fat

BAKED APPLE

2 small apples
1 pkt sweetener
Dash cinnamon and nutmeg
1/4 cup water
1 tsp lemon juice

Core apples and place in baking dish. Sprinkle sweetener, cinnamon and nutmeg on apples. Add water and lemon juice to baking dish.

Bake 450⁰F. for 25 minutes, or until apples are tender.

Serves 2.

Per Serving:

Nutrition Information		Exchanges	
cal	60	frt	1
pro	0gm		
carb	16gm		
fat	0gm		
satfat	0gm		
chol	0mg		
sod	4mg		

0% of calories from fat
0% of calories from saturated fat

DREAMY FRUIT

1 cup canned fruit cocktail, no sugar added
1/2 cup nonfat dry milk powder
3 pkts EQUAL
1/4 tsp vanilla

Drain liquid from fruit cocktail into a medium mixing bowl, reserving fruit. Add remaining ingredients and beat with an electric mixer until smooth. Gently fold in fruit. Serve at once.

Serves 2.

Per Serving:

Nutrition Information		Exchanges	
cal	114	milk	3/4
pro	8gm	frt	3/4
carb	23gm		
fat	0gm		
satfat	0gm		
chol	3mg		
sod	96mg		

0% of calories from fat
0% of calories from saturated fat

AMBROSIA WHIP

1 cup skim milk
2 tab frozen orange juice concentrate
1 tsp coconut extract
6 ice cubes
Orange rind garnish (optional)

Combine skim milk, orange juice concentrate and extract in blender. Process until foamy. Add ice cubes, one at a time, blending after each addition until very thick. Pour into a chilled glass. Garnish with orange rind if desired.

Serves 1.

Per Serving:

Nutrition Information		Exchanges	
cal	142	milk	1
pro	9gm	frt	1
carb	25gm		
fat	<1gm		
satfat	<1gm		
chol	4mg		
sod	127mg		

3% of calories from fat
2% of calories from saturated fat

ORANGE WHIP

1/4 cup cold water
1 envelope unflavored gelatin
2 cups orange juice
3 pkts EQUAL
1/2 tsp vanilla

In a saucepan, sprinkle gelatin over water to soften. Add orange juice. Cook over medium heat about 5 minutes or until gelatin is completely dissolved. Remove from heat and stir in EQUAL and vanilla. Place mixture in bowl and beat with electric mixer until light and fluffy. Spoon into dessert dishes and chill until firm.

Serves 4.

Per Serving:

Nutrition Information		Exchanges	
cal	67	frt	1
pro	2gm		
carb	14gm		
fat	0gm		
satfat	0gm		
chol	0mg		
sod	3mg		

0% of calories from fat
0% of calories from saturated fat

CHOCOLATE MINT FREEZE

3/4 cup buttermilk
1/2 cup crushed pineapple with juice, no sugar added
3 pkts EQUAL
1 tsp chocolate extract
1/8 tsp peppermint extract

In a bowl combine all ingredients and mix well. Freeze about 3 hours or until slightly frozen.

Serves 1.

Per Serving:

Nutrition Information		Exchanges	
cal	156	fat	1/2
pro	6gm	milk	3/4
carb	3gm	frt	1
fat	<2gm		
satfat	1gm		
chol	7mg		
sod	203mg		

9% of calories from fat
6% of calories from saturated fat

ANGEL CLOUDS

1/2 cup water
1 cup nonfat dry milk powder
3/4 cup orange juice
8 pkts EQUAL
2 tsp sherry extract
1/2 tsp almond extract
1/2 tsp vanilla
Orange rind to garnish

Combine water and nonfat dry milk powder in bowl; beat with electric mixer until thickened. Add orange juice and beat an additional 5 minutes or until thickened. Add EQUAL and beat until consistency of whipped cream. Fold in extracts. Divide evenly into dessert dishes and garnish with a slice of orange rind.

Serves 6.

Per Serving:

Nutrition Information		Exchanges	
cal	61	milk	1/2
pro	4gm	frt	1/4
carb	11gm		
fat	0gm		
satfat	0gm		
chol	2mg		
sod	63mg		

0% of calories from fat
0% of calories from saturated fat

PINEAPPLE DELITE

1/4 cup cold water
1 envelope unflavored gelatin
1/4 cup boiling water
1/2 cup crushed pineapple with juice, no sugar added
1/3 cup nonfat dry milk powder
1/2 tsp vanilla or pineapple extract
3 pkts EQUAL
5 - 6 ice cubes

Put cold water in blender, sprinkle gelatin over cold water to soften. Add boiling water, 3/4 of the pineapple, dry milk powder, extract and EQUAL. Blend until smooth. Add ice cubes one at a time, blending after each addition. Fold in remaining pineapple and put into serving dish.

Serves 1.

Per Serving:

Nutrition Information		Exchanges	
cal	187	milk	1
pro	13gm	frt	1
carb	32gm		
fat	0gm		
satfat	0gm		
chol	4mg		
sod	133mg		

0% of calories from fat
0% of calories from saturated fat

PINEAPPLE FLUFF

3/4 cup buttermilk
1/2 cup crushed pineapple, own juice no sugar added
1 pkt EQUAL (optional)
1/2 tsp vanilla

Combine all ingredients in a small bowl. Pour into a dessert dish or parfait glass and freeze about 2 to 3 hours. Allow dessert to set at room temperature 5 to 10 minutes before serving.

Serves 1.

Per Serving:

Nutrition Information		Exchanges	
cal	155	fat	1/2
pro	6gm	milk	3/4
carb	28gm	frt	1
fat	<2gm		
satfat	1gm		
chol	7mg		
sod	203mg		

9% of calories from fat
6% of calories from saturated fat

PINEAPPLE CHEESE BAKLAVA

1/2 can (20 oz) crushed pineapple own juice, no sugar added
8 oz reduced calorie cream cheese
1 cup part skim ricotta cheese
1/4 cup fructose or 1/3 cup granulated sugar replacement
1/4 cup Eggbeaters
1 tsp vanilla
1/2 lb Fillo dough
1/2 cup melted diet imitation margarine
1 tsp arrowroot

Drain pineapple and save juice. In mixing bowl combine cream cheese, ricotta cheese, fructose, Eggbeaters and vanilla. Mix together on medium speed with electric mixer.

Stir in drained pineapple. Place Fillo dough in wax paper and cover with damp (not wet) towel to keep moist or in large plastic storage bag (i.e., Glad or Baggie)

Place 1 sheet of Fillo dough in jellyroll pan (9 x 13 x 2) sprayed with release agent. Brush lightly with melted margarine. Repeat with 8 - 12 sheets.

Spoon the pineapple-cheese mixture on the Fillo dough and spread evenly. Top with remaining Fillo, brushing with melted margarine.

Cut into diamonds on top of dough only (electric knife works best). Bake at 350°F. 50 minutes, or until golden brown.

Combine 1/2 cup pineapple juice and arrowroot. Cook to thick syrup. When baklava is baked, spoon hot syrup evenly over the top. Cool completely (can be refrigerated after partially cooled). Then finish cutting into diamonds at markings.

Store refrigerated. Can be frozen.

PINEAPPLE CHEESE BAKLAVA
(continued)

Serves 48.

Per Serving (1 piece):

Nutrition Information		Exchanges	
cal	47	pro	1/4
pro	2gm	brd	1/4
carb	4gm	fat	1/2
fat	2gm		
satfat	<1gm		
chol	2mg		
sod	43mg		

76% of calories from fat
8% of calories from saturated fat

STRAWBERRY COBBLER

    2 cups strawberries
    1/2 cup + 2 tab water
    2 tab cornstarch
    1 tsp strawberry extract
    2 pkts sweetener

Slice strawberries and set aside. In saucepan combine water and cornstarch, cook stirring constantly until mixture thickens and boils. Boil and stir 1 more minute. Remove from heat, add strawberries, extract and sweetener. Pour into 1-1/2 qt. casserole.

Stir together:
    10 tab flour
    1-1/4 tsp baking powder
    2 pkts sweetener

Cut in:
    2 tab diet imitation margarine
    1/4 cup skim milk

Drop dough in 4 equal parts on top of hot fruit. Bake 25-30 minutes at 400ºF. or until biscuit topping is golden brown.

Serves 4.

Per Serving:

Nutrition Information		Exchanges	
cal	148	brd	1-1/4
pro	3gm	fat	2/3
carb	26gm	frt	1/2
fat	3gm		
satfat	<1gm		
chol	0mg		
sod	185mg		

18% of calories from fat
3% of calories from saturated fat

PEACH COBBLER

2 cups sliced peaches (canned in own juice, no sugar added), with 1 cup juice
1/2 tsp cinnamon
4 tab cornstarch

In saucepan combine peaches, juice, cinnamon and cornstarch. Cook stirring constantly until mixture thickens and boils. Boil and stir 1 more minute. Pour into 1-1/2 qt. casserole.

Stir together:
10 tab flour
1-1/4 tsp baking powder
2 pkts sweetener

Cut in:
2 tab diet imitation margarine
1/4 cup skim milk

Drop dough in 4 equal parts on top of hot fruit. Bake 25-30 minutes at 400°F. or until biscuit topping is golden brown.

Serves 4.

Per Serving:

Nutrition Information		Exchanges	
cal	156	brd	1-1/2
pro	3gm	fat	2/3
carb	29gm	frt	1/2
fat	3gm		
satfat	<1gm		
chol	0mg		
sod	185mg		

17% of calories from fat
3% of calories from saturated fat

RICE PUDDING

3 cups cooked rice
3 cups skim milk
3/4 cup raisins
1 tsp vanilla
Sweetener to equal 1/3 cup sugar (8 pkts)

Cook rice, milk and raisins over medium heat, stirring occasionally, until thick and creamy (about 15 minutes). Remove from heat, stir in vanilla and sweetener. Cool.

Serves 6.

Per Serving:

Nutrition Information		Exchanges	
cal	215	brd	1-1/2
pro	7gm	milk	1/2
carb	47gm	frt	1
fat	0gm		
satfat	0gm		
chol	2mg		
sod	68mg		

0% of calories from fat
0% of calories from saturated fat

PUMPKIN PINEAPPLE PUDDING

1/2 cup pumpkin, no sugar added
1/2 cup crushed pineapple with juice, no sugar added
1/4 cup Eggbeaters
1/3 cup nonfat dry milk powder
2 tab brown sugar replacement
1 tsp cinnamon
1 tsp vanilla
1/8 tsp nutmeg
1/8 tsp allspice
2 egg whites
1/8 tsp cream of tartar

Combine pumpkin, crushed pineapple, Eggbeaters, dry milk powder, brown sugar replacement, cinnamon, vanilla, nutmeg and allspice; mix well. Beat egg whites with cream of tartar until stiff peaks form. Fold egg whites into pumpkin-pineapple mixture. Pour into 2-1/2 qt. glass baking casserole sprayed with release agent. Bake at 350ºF. 25 minutes or until cooked throughout.

Serves 2.

Per Serving:

Nutrition Information		Exchanges	
cal	137	pro	1
pro	10gm	brd	1/2
carb	23gm	milk	1/2
fat	0gm	frt	1/2
satfat	0gm		
chol	2mg		
sod	160mg		

0% of calories from fat
0% of calories from saturated fat

STRAWBERRY PUDDING

1/2 cup cold water
2 envelopes unflavored gelatin
1 cup skim milk, heated to boiling
6 pkts EQUAL
1 tsp strawberry extract
1 quart fresh strawberries, washed and hulled

Put water in blender container. Sprinkle gelatin over water and let stand 3 to 4 minutes. Add hot milk and blend at low speed until gelatin is completely dissolved (approximately 2 minutes). Add remaining ingredients and blend on high speed until strawberries are pureed. Pour into dessert dishes and chill until set.

Serves 8.

Per Serving:

Nutrition Information		Exchanges	
cal	43	milk	1/8
pro	3gm	frt	1/2
carb	7gm		
fat	0gm		
satfat	0gm		
chol	1mg		
sod	19mg		

0% of calories from fat
0% of calories from saturated fat

TRIFLE

1 pkg sugar free lemon or pound cake mix
  (one 8 or 9 inch layer)
1 pkg sugar free vanilla pudding
2 cups skim milk
1/2 cup Cool Whip
1 medium banana, sliced
2 cups strawberries, sliced
2 pkts EQUAL or to taste

Bake cake according to package directions. Allow to cool thoroughly. Turn cake onto cutting board and cut in half horizontally, then into bite size squares.

Mix vanilla pudding and skim milk according to pudding directions. Fold in Cool Whip to consistancy of custard. In a separate bowl, mix sliced banana, strawberries, and EQUAL together.

In a desert or trifle bowl, alternate layers of cake, fruit, and pudding mixture. Let stand at least 2 hours before serving. Store refrigerated.

Serves 10.

Per Serving:

Nutrition Information		Exchanges	
cal	156	brd	1
pro	3gm	fat	1/2
carb	28gm	milk	1/4
fat	3gm	frt	1/3
satfat	0gm		
chol	1mg		
sod	218mg		

17% of calories from fat
0% of calories from saturated fat

Note: Can substitute 2 cups fruit cocktail drained, for fresh fruit.

Notes:

CAKES

APRICOT UPSIDE-DOWN CAKE

12 fresh or frozen apricot halves, thawed
1/2 tsp lemon juice
1/2 tab brown sugar replacement
1/4 tsp cinnamon
2 slices white bread made into crumbs
1 tsp baking powder
1/4 cup Eggbeaters
1/3 cup granulated sugar replacement
3 tab hot water
1/2 tsp vanilla
2 egg whites

Preheat oven to 350ºF. In medium bowl combine apricots, lemon juice, brown sugar replacement and cinnamon. Spread on bottom of non-stick baking pan. Combine bread crumbs and baking powder and set aside. Beat Eggbeaters and gradually add granulated sugar replacement beating until thick and lemon colored. Beat in the hot water, bread crumb mixture and vanilla. In a small bowl, beat egg whites until stiff but not dry and fold into the Eggbeaters mixture. Pour over the apricots. Bake about 25 minutes or until cooked throughout.

Serves 2.

Per Serving:

Nutrition Information   Exchanges

cal	163	pro	1
pro	9gm	brd	3/4
carb	29gm	fat	1/4
fat	1gm	frt	1
satfat	0gm		
chol	0mg		
sod	395mg		

6% of calories from fat
0% of calories from saturated fat

FRUITED CHEESECAKE

Graham Cracker Crust: see Index.

Filling: (Note: Crust must be chilled)

>	20 oz can pineapple chunks in own juice, no
>		sugar added
>	Water
>	1 pkg sugar free lemon gelatin (4, 1/2 cup
>		servings size)
>	8 oz pkg imitation or reduced calorie cream cheese,
>		softened to room temperature
>	1 pkt EQUAL

Drain pineapple chunks and reserve juice. Chill the pineapple. Add water to pineapple juice to make 1 cup and bring to boil in a small saucepan. Remove from heat. Add lemon gelatin and stir until gelatin is completely dissolved. In small bowl, beat cream cheese and EQUAL with electric mixer. Gradually add half of the gelatin mixture to the cream cheese, beating until smooth. Pour into chilled pie crust. Chill until set.

When pie is set, arrange pineapple chunks on top of pie and spoon rest of gelatin mixture over all. Chill.

Serves 8.

Per Serving:

Nutrition Information		Exchanges	
cal	195	pro	1
pro	9gm	brd	1/2
carb	21gm	fat	1-1/2
fat	8gm	frt	1/2
satfat	<1gm		
chol	0mg		
sod	146mg		

37% of calories from fat
2% of calories from saturated fat

Note: Can also use canned peaches in own juice, in place of pineapple.

PLAIN CHEESECAKE

Graham Cracker Crust:

> 16 graham crackers, made into crumbs
> 8 tsp diet imitation margarine

Melt margarine. Add margarine to graham cracker crumbs and mix thoroughly. Press into 9 inch pie plate. Bake 350ºF. for 10 minutes until lightly browned. Chill.

Filling: (Note: Crust must be chilled)

> 1 cup water
> 1 pkg sugar free lemon gelatin (4, 1/2 cup servings size)
> 8 oz pkg imitation or reduced calorie cream cheese,
>   softened to room temperature
> 1 pkt EQUAL

In small saucepan, bring 1 cup water to boil. Remove from heat. Add lemon gelatin and stir until gelatin is completely dissolved. In small bowl, beat cream cheese and EQUAL with electric mixer. Gradually add half of the hot gelatin mixture to the cream cheese, beating until smooth. Pour into chilled pie crust. Chill until set.

When pie is set, gently pour rest of the gelatin mixture over top and chill.

Serves 8.

Per Serving:

Nutrition Information		Exchanges	
cal	151	pro	1
pro	9gm	brd	1/2
carb	10gm	fat	1-1/2
fat	8gm		
satfat	<1gm		
chol	0mg		
sod	140mg		

48% of calories from fat
3% of calories from saturated fat

QUICK AND EASY CHEESECAKE

Graham Cracker Crust: see Index.

Filling: (Note: Crust must be chilled)

    1 envelope unflavored gelatin
    1 cup boiling water
    2 8 oz pkg imitation or reduced calorie cream cheese,
        softened to room temperature
    1 tsp vanilla
    Sweetener to equal 1/2 cup sugar

Put gelatin in large bowl, add boiling water and stir until gelatin is completely dissolved. With electric mixer, beat in cream cheese, vanilla and sweetener until smooth. Pour into chilled prepared graham cracker crust and chill until firm, about 2 hours.

Serves 8.

Per Serving:

Nutrition Information		Exchanges	
cal	227	pro	2
pro	16gm	brd	1/2
carb	10gm	fat	2-1/2
fat	13gm		
satfat	<1gm		
chol	0mg		
sod	111mg		

52% of calories from fat
2% of calories from saturated fat

FRUIT COCKTAIL CAKE

1 16 oz can fruit cocktail, no sugar added
1 tsp (heaping) baking soda
1 cup granulated sugar replacement
1/4 cup non-fat dry powdered milk
1/4 cup Eggbeaters
1 cup flour
1/2 tsp vanilla
Brown sugar replacement

Spray one 8 inch square cake pan with release agent. In mixing bowl add baking soda to fruit cocktail mixing well. Combine all ingredients except brown sugar replacement and mix well. Pour into cake pan and sprinkle with brown sugar replacement. Bake at 350ºF. for approximately 25 minutes or until done.

Serves 6.

Per Serving:

Nutrition Information		Exchanges	
cal	129	pro	1/4
pro	5gm	brd	1
carb	27gm	frt	1/2
fat	0gm		
satfat	0gm		
chol	1mg		
sod	170mg		

0% of calories from fat
0% of calories from saturated fat

CARROT CAKE

1/2 cup Eggbeaters
1/3 cup granulated sugar replacement
1/3 cup granulated fructose
1/4 cup unsaturated vegetable oil
1/2 cup crushed pineapple own juice, no sugar added
1-1/2 cups grated carrots
1-1/2 cups flour
1-1/2 tsp baking powder
1 tsp baking soda
1 tsp cinnamon

In a large bowl beat Eggbeaters with wire whisk. Add sugar replacement, fructose and oil. Beat well. Add pineapple and carrots, mixing thoroughly with wooden spoon. Sift together flour, baking powder, baking soda and cinnamon. Add dry ingredients to mixture and mix thoroughly.

Option 1. Fill miniature muffin tins sprayed with release agent or line with paper baking cups. Bake 400ºF. about 20 minutes until golden in color.

Yield: 40 miniature muffins

Serves 20.

Per Serving (2 muffins):

Nutrition Information		Exchanges	
cal	78	veg	1/4
pro	2gm	brd	1/2
carb	9gm	fat	1/2
fat	3gm		
satfat	<1gm		
chol	0mg		
sod	78mg		

35% of calories from fat
4% of calories from saturated fat

CARROT CAKE
(Continued)

Option 2. Pour into 9 X 13 X 2 baking tray and bake 400ºF. about 35 minutes or until golden.

Serves 18.

Per Serving (1 piece):

Nutrition Information		Exchanges	
cal	87	veg	1/4
pro	2gm	brd	1/2
carb	10gm	fat	1/2
fat	3gm		
satfat	1gm		
chol	0mg		
sod	87mg		

31% of calories from fat
4% of calories from saturated fat

FRUIT CAKE

2-1/2 cups flour
1 tsp baking soda
1 tsp baking powder
1-1/2 tsp ginger
1-1/2 tsp cinnamon
1-1/2 tsp allspice
1/2 cup nonfat mayonnaise
1/2 cup granulated fructose
1/2 cup Eggbeaters
2 tsp rum extract
1 cup applesauce, no sugar added
2 cups dried fruit chopped (raisins, dates,
    prunes, apricots) 1/2 cup each
1 cup chopped walnuts

Mix together flour, baking soda, baking powder, ginger, cinnamon, allspice and set aside. In large mixer bowl cream mayonnaise and fructose. Add Eggbeaters and rum extract, beat well. Add flour mixture alternately with applesauce. Mix dried fruits and nuts together and fold into batter.

Option 1. Pour into 2 loaf pans (7 1/2 X 3 1/2 X 2) sprayed with release agent and lightly floured. Bake at 325ºF. 1 to 1-1/4 hours. Remove from pans and cool on rack. Cut 16 slices per loaf.

Serves 32.

Per Serving (1 slice):

Nutrition Information		Exchanges	
cal	104	brd	1/2
pro	2gm	fat	1/2
carb	16gm	frt	1/2
fat	2gm		
satfat	<1gm		
chol	0mg		
sod	74mg		

17% of calories from fat
2% of calories from saturated fat

FRUIT CAKE
(Continued)

Option 2. Fill miniature muffin tins lined with paper cups or sprayed with release agent. Bake at 325⁰F. 25 minutes. Yield 5 dozen.

Serves 60.

Per Serving (1 mini muffin):

Nutrition Information		Exchanges	
cal	55	brd	1/3
pro	1gm	fat	1/4
carb	9gm	frt	1/3
fat	1gm		
satfat	0gm		
chol	0mg		
sod	39mg		

16% of calories from fat
2% of calories from saturated fat

Note: Fruit cake should be wrapped and stored in a cool place at least 24 hours before serving. Freezes well.

PINA COLADA CAKE

1 cup less 1 tab flour
1 tsp baking powder
1/4 cup diet imitation margarine
3 to 4 tab cold water
2 cups crushed pineapple own juice, no sugar added
2 tab cornstarch
2 tsp vanilla
2 tsp rum extract
3 egg whites
1/4 tsp cream of tartar
Sweetener to equal 3 tsp sugar
2 tab + 2 tsp shredded unsweetened coconut

Preheat oven to 400°F.

CRUST: Combine flour and baking powder in a medium bowl, cut in margarine until coarse crumbs form. Add water gradually until ball forms. Pat into bottom of 8 inch square pan sprayed with release agent. Bake 10 minutes, set aside to cool.

FILLING: In a medium saucepan combine crushed pineapple with cornstarch and extracts. Stir over medium heat until thickened. Pour into crust.

TOPPING: In a small bowl, using electric mixer on high, beat egg whites, cream of tartar and sweetener until stiff but not dry. Spread over pineapple mixture. Sprinkle coconut evenly on top. Bake about 10 min. or until golden brown. Cool on wire rack.

Serves 9.

Per Serving:

Nutrition Information		Exchanges	
cal	129	brd	1
pro	3gm	fat	1
carb	21gm	frt	1/2
fat	3gm		
satfat	1gm		
chol	0mg		
sod	123mg		

21% of calories from fat
7% of calories from saturated fat

PUMPKIN CAKE

    2 cups flour
    3 tsp baking powder
    2 tsp baking soda
    2 tsp cinnamon
    1 tsp ginger
    4 egg whites
    2/3 cup granulated fructose
    1 cup unsaturated vegetable oil
    2 cups pumpkin

In mixing bowl combine all ingredients and mix well with electric mixer. Pour into 9 X 13 pan that has been sprayed with release agent. Bake at 350ºF. 40 minutes. Top with Cream Cheese Frosting if desired.

Serves 18.

Per Serving:

Nutrition Information		Exchanges	
cal	192	brd	1
pro	3gm	fat	2-1/2
carb	13gm		
fat	12gm		
satfat	<2gm		
chol	0mg		
sod	162mg		

56% of calories from fat
8% of calories from saturated fat

Freezes well.

CREAM CHEESE FROSTING

1/2 cup diet imitation margarine
8 oz reduced calorie cream cheese
2 cups Powdered Sugar replacement with fructose
   (see index)
1 tsp vanilla

Soften margarine and cream cheese to room temperature. In mixing bowl, combine all ingredients and beat well with electric mixer. After cake is cool, spread frosting over the cake and refrigerate. The flavor enhances when cake is refrigerated at least overnight before serving.

Serves 18.

Per Serving:

Nutrition Information		Exchanges	
cal	105	pro	1/2
pro	4gm	brd	1/2
carb	8gm	fat	1
fat	5gm	milk	1/4
satfat	<1gm		
chol	1mg		
sod	79mg		

43% of calories from fat
4% of calories from saturated fat

PIES

DEEP DISH APPLE PIE

14 small apples peeled, cored and sliced (3-1/2 pounds)
1 tsp cinnamon
1 tsp coconut extract
4 tsp vanilla
4 pkts sweetener
1/4 cup water

Mix above ingredients in sauce pan and simmer until apples are tender. Stir frequently.

2 envelopes unflavored gelatin
1 cup water

In small bowl dissolve 2 envelopes unflavored gelatin in 1/2 cup cold water, then add 1/2 cup hot water. Add to mixture in saucepan. Pour into 8'' square pan that has been sprayed with release agent.

TOPPING:

2/3 cup nonfat powdered milk dry
2 pkts sweetener
1 tsp cinnamon

Mix together and sprinkle over pie. Bake 350ºF. 20 minutes. Cool 1/2 hour and refrigerate.

Serves 8.

Per Serving:

Nutrition Information		Exchanges	
cal	141	milk	1/4
pro	2gm	frt	2
carb	33gm		
fat	<1gm		
satfat	0gm		
chol	1mg		
sod	31mg		

4% of calories from fat
0% of calories from saturated fat

APPLE PIE

Graham Cracker Crust: see Index

Note: Crust must be chilled

Mix together in large bowl — 2-1/2 qts (microwave proof, or pan for stove):

       1 12 oz can frozen apple juice concentrate, undiluted
       2 tab cornstarch
       1 tsp cinnamon
       1/2 tsp nutmeg

ADD:

       6 yellow delicious apples, cored and sliced (peeled or
         unpeeled — your preference)
       2 tab diet imitation margarine

MICROWAVE DIRECTIONS: Cover with wax paper or glass cover and microwave on high 8 minutes, stir after 4 minutes. Remove cover and cook additional 8 minutes, stirring after 4 minutes.

STOVE DIRECTIONS: Cook mixture until apples are tender and sauce is thickened.

Let cool, pour into chilled crust and refrigerate.

Serves 8.

Per Serving:

Nutrition Information		Exchanges	
cal	188	brd	1
pro	1gm	fat	1
carb	37gm	frt	1-1/2
fat	5gm		
satfat	<1gm		
chol	0mg		
sod	148mg		

24% of calories from fat
4% of calories from saturated fat

AMBROSIA PIE

2 cups crushed pineapple (own juice no sugar added)
1 cup mandarin oranges (own juice no sugar added)
3 envelopes unflavored gelatin
3 cups plain nonfat yogurt
3 tsp coconut extract
Sweetener to taste
6 2-1/2 inch graham cracker squares made into crumbs
4 tsp unsweetened shredded coconut

In saucepan, drain juice from fruits, add gelatin and heat until gelatin is dissolved. Remove from heat. Add fruits and stir well. Stir in yogurt, extract and sweetener. Pour into desired mold or pie plate.

Refrigerate until firm. At serving time, top with graham cracker crumbs and coconut.

Serves 6.

Per Serving:

Nutrition Information		Exchanges	
cal	168	brd	1/3
pro	10gm	fat	1/3
carb	29gm	milk	3/4
fat	1gm	frt	3/4
satfat	<1gm		
chol	2mg		
sod	137mg		

5% of calories from fat
3% of calories from saturated fat

BANANA CREAM PIE I

1/2 banana
1 cup crushed pineapple (own juice, no sugar added)

Slice banana very thin in a 9 inch pie plate. Drain pineapple and reserve juice. Spread pineapple on top of banana.

In blender:
Add reserved pineapple juice
1 envelope unflavored gelatin
MIX on medium

Add 1/2 cup HOT orange juice
MIX again

Add 1-1/3 cups dry milk powder
1/2 cup water
Sweetener to equal 1 tab sugar
1 tsp vanilla (optional) (could also use coconut or almond extract)
MIX well — 3 to 4 minutes

Pour over banana and crushed pineapple and refrigerate.

Serves 4.

Per Serving:

Nutrition Information		Exchanges	
cal	153	milk	1
pro	10gm	frt	1
carb	28gm		
fat	0gm		
satfat	0gm		
chol	4mg		
sod	132mg		

0% of calories from fat
0% of calories from saturated fat

BANANA CREAM PIE II

Graham Cracker Crust: see Index

Note: Crust must be chilled

    2 bananas sliced into pie crust
    1 pkg Jello sugar-free Vanilla Pudding (4 1/2 cup serving
      size)
    1-3/4 cups skim milk

Using a wire whisk, mix pudding and milk together for 60 seconds. The pie will break down if beat longer. Immediately pour pudding over bananas and chill.

Serves 6.

Per Serving:

Nutrition Information		Exchanges	
cal	176	brd	1
pro	5gm	fat	3/4
carb	30gm	milk	1/3
fat	4gm	frt	1/2
satfat	<1gm		
chol	1mg		
sod	401mg		

20% of calories from fat
4% of calories from saturated fat

PISTACHIO PIE

Graham Cracker Crust: see Index

Note: Crust must be chilled

    1 pkg Jello sugar-free Pistachio Pudding (4-1/2 cup serving size)
    1-3/4 cups skim milk

Using a wire whisk, mix pudding and milk together for 60 seconds. The pie will break down if beat longer. Immediately pour pudding into crust and chill.

Serves 6.

Per Serving:

Nutrition Information		Exchanges	
cal	144	brd	1
pro	4gm	fat	1
carb	21gm	milk	1/3
fat	5gm		
satfat	<1gm		
chol	1mg		
sod	400mg		

31% of calories from fat
5% of calories from saturated fat

STRAWBERRY GLAZE PIE

Graham Cracker Crust: see Index

Note: Crust must be chilled

> 1 qt fresh strawberries
> Equal sweetener (optional)
> 1 pkg Strawberry Jello sugar-free (4-1/2 cup serving size)
> 1-1/4 cups boiling water

Wash, hull and slice strawberries into a bowl. Add Equal to strawberries if desired, and refrigerate. Mix Jello in boiling water and refrigerate until slightly set. Mix strawberries and Jello together and pour into pie crust. If Jello is not set enough, the crust will get soggy.

Serves 6.

Per Serving:

Nutrition Information		Exchanges	
cal	131	brd	3/4
pro	3gm	fat	3/4
carb	20gm	frt	1/2
fat	4gm		
satfat	<1gm		
chol	0mg		
sod	187mg		

27% of calories from fat
5% of calories from saturated fat

STRAWBERRY PIE

In blender:

> 4 oz diet 7UP or diet Red Pop
> 2 envelopes unflavored gelatin
> MIX together on high

> Add 1/2 cup boiling water
> MIX again

> Add 1-1/3 cups dry milk powder
> 1 tsp strawberry extract
> Sweetener to equal 1 tsp sugar (EQUAL is best)
> 2 cups strawberries (whole)

MIX all together

Pour into pie plate and refrigerate.

Serves 4.

Per Serving:

Nutrition Information		Exchanges	
cal	115	milk	1
pro	11gm	frt	1/2
carb	17gm		
fat	0gm		
satfat	0gm		
chol	4mg		
sod	129mg		

0% of calories from fat
0% of calories from saturated fat

Note: Can use crushed graham crackers for a crust — 3 crackers
(2-1/2 inch square) count as 1 bread (80 calories)

PINEAPPLE PIE

16 oz can crushed pineapple, own juice no sugar added
1 tsp cinnamon
1 tsp coconut extract
2 tsp vanilla
1 tab lemon juice
1 pkt sweetener
2 envelopes unflavored gelatin

In a saucepan mix all ingredients except gelatin and simmer 10 minutes. In a small bowl dissolve gelatin in 1/2 cup cold water and then add 1/2 cup hot water. Add to mixture in saucepan. Pour into a 9 inch pie plate.

TOPPING:

2/3 cup nonfat powdered milk dry
2 pkts sweetener
1 tsp cinnamon

Mix together and sprinkle over pie. Bake pie at 350°F. for 20 minutes. Cool 30 minutes and refrigerate.

Serves 4.

Per Serving:

Nutrition Information		Exchanges	
cal	133	milk	1/2
pro	7gm	frt	1
carb	26gm		
fat	0gm		
satfat	0gm		
chol	2mg		
sod	74mg		

0% of calories from fat
0% of calories from saturated fat

PUMPKIN PIE

16 oz can pumpkin, no sugar added
13 oz can evaporated skim milk
2 envelopes unflavored gelatin
1 tsp cinnamon
1 tsp pumpkin pie spice
Sweetener to equal 1 tab sugar

Mix all ingredients together and pour into pie plate. Bake 425ºF. for 20 minutes. Reduce heat to 375ºF. and bake additional 20 minutes.

Serves 4.

Per Serving:

Nutrition Information		Exchanges	
cal	128	brd	1/2
pro	11gm	milk	1
carb	21gm		
fat	<1gm		
satfat	<1gm		
chol	4mg		
sod	118mg		

4% of calories from fat
2% of calories from saturated fat

WHIPPED CREAM SUBSTITUTE TOPPING

Beat together about 10 minutes:
      1/2 cup diet 7UP
      2 envelopes unflavored gelatin

Add
      1/4 cup boiling water
      1/3 cup nonfat dry milk powder

Keep beating until mixture peaks.

Serves 4.

Per Serving:

Nutrition Information		Exchanges	
cal	31	milk	1/4
pro	5gm		
carb	3gm		
fat	0gm		
satfat	0gm		
chol	1mg		
sod	34mg		

0% of calories from fat
0% of calories from saturated fat

PUMPKIN CHIFFON PIE

Graham Cracker Crust: see Index.

Filling: (Note: Crust must be chilled)

      1 pkg vanilla sugar-free pudding mix
         (4 - 1/2 cup serving size)
      3/4 cup skim milk
      1/2 cup solid pack pumpkin, no sugar added
      1/2 tsp allspice
      1/2 tsp ginger
      1/8 tsp nutmeg
      2 cups Cool Whip

Put skim milk and pudding mix in mixing bowl and beat with wire whisk for 1 minute. Mixture will be very thick. Set aside and let stand for 5 minutes. In another bowl, mix together pumpkin, allspice, ginger and nutmeg. With a large spoon (wooden) blend pumpkin mixture into pudding. Fold in Cool Whip. Spoon into chilled pie crust. Chill 4 hours before serving.

Recipe can be multiplied. For a 10 x 3 spring form pan, double the recipe.

Serves 8.

Per Serving:

Nutrition Information		Exchanges	
cal	122	brd	1
pro	2gm	fat	1/2
carb	18gm		
fat	5gm		
satfat	<1gm		
chol	0mg		
sod	282mg		

37% of calories from fat
4% of calories from saturated fat

COOKIES

APPLESAUCE COOKIES

2 cups flour
1 cup quick oats, uncooked
1 tsp baking soda
1 tsp cinnamon
1 tsp ginger
1 tsp allspice
1 cup diet imitation margarine
1 cup brown sugar replacement
1/3 cup granulated fructose
2 egg whites or 1/4 cup Eggbeaters
1 tsp vanilla
1 cup applesauce, no sugar added
1 cup raisins, chopped if desired

Combine flour, oats, baking soda, cinnamon, ginger and allspice. In large mixer bowl, cream margarine. Gradually add brown sugar replacement and fructose, beating until light and fluffy. Add egg whites and vanilla. Alternate additions of dry ingredients with applesauce mixing well after each addition. Fold in raisins. Drop by teaspoonfuls on cookie sheet sprayed with release agent and spread to desired shape. Bake at 350°F. about 25 minutes until cookies are lightly browned and firm.

Yield: 80 cookies

Serves 40.

Per Serving (2 cookies):

Nutrition Information		Exchanges	
cal	72	brd	1/2
pro	1gm	fat	1/2
carb	10gm	frt	1/4
fat	2gm		
satfat	<1gm		
chol	0mg		
sod	76mg		

25% of calories from fat
6% of calories from saturated fat

Freezes well.

BROWNIES

1/2 cup stone ground whole wheat flour (see variation below)
1/2 tsp baking powder
1/4 cup diet imitation margarine
1/2 cup honey
1/4 cup carob powder
2 egg whites or 1/4 cup Eggbeaters
1/4 cup walnut pieces
1/2 tsp vanilla

Use a wire whisk for all mixing. Sift together flour and baking powder, set aside. In a small saucepan melt margarine over low heat. Add honey, mix, then add carob powder. Mix until thoroughly blended. Remove from heat. In medium mixing bowl, beat egg whites lightly; gradually add carob mixture to egg whites. Add dry ingredients and mix well. Blend in vanilla and walnuts. Pour into 8 X 8 square pan that has been sprayed with release agent. Bake at 350ºF. about 25 minutes or until wooden pick inserted in center comes out clean. Cool before cutting into 16 pieces.

Variation: Replace wheat flour with 2/3 cup oat flour. After putting batter in pan, let stand for about 20 minutes before baking.

Serves 16.

Per Serving:

Nutrition Information		Exchanges	
cal	80	brd	1/3
pro	2gm	fat	1/3
carb	14gm		
fat	2gm		
satfat	<1gm		
chol	0mg		
sod	51mg		

26% of calories from fat
3% of calories from saturated fat

Freezes well.

CAROB CHIP COOKIES

    2 cups flour
    2 tsp baking powder
    1 cup diet imitation margarine
    1/2 cup brown sugar replacement
    1/3 cup granulated fructose
    2 egg whites, beaten but not stiff
    1/2 cup skim milk
    1 tsp vanilla
    1 cup unsweetened carob chips
    1/2 cup chopped walnuts

Sift flour and baking powder. Cream margarine with brown sugar replacement and fructose until light and fluffy. Add egg whites and mix well at medium speed. Combine milk and vanilla, and add alternately with flour mixture. Mix thoroughly. Stir in carob chips and nuts. Drop by teaspoonfuls onto baking sheet that has been sprayed with release agent. Bake at 350°F. about 15 minutes or until edges are browned.

Yield: 6 dozen cookies

Serves 72.

Per Serving (1 cookie):

Nutrition Information		Exchanges	
cal	53	brd	1/4
pro	1gm	fat	1/3
carb	12gm		
fat	2gm		
satfat	<1gm		
chol	0mg		
sod	41mg		

34% of calories from fat
5% of calories from saturated fat

Freezes well.

OATMEAL COOKIES

1 cup Basic Baking Mix (see Index) or Reduced Fat
   Bisquick
1/2 cup quick oats, uncooked
1/2 tsp cinnamon
1/3 cup brown sugar replacement
Sweetener to equal 1/3 cup sugar
1/4 cup raisins, chopped
8 dried apricots, chopped
1/4 tsp vanilla
1/3 cup water or a little more if needed

In a large bowl, mix all ingredients together well. Drop by teaspoonfuls on cookie sheet sprayed with release agent. Bake at 350ºF. about 15 minutes until done.

Yield: 24 cookies

Serves 12.

Per Serving (2 cookies):

Nutrition Information		Exchanges	
cal	80	brd	1/2
pro	2gm	fat	1/3
carb	15gm	frt	1/2
fat	2gm		
satfat	<1gm		
chol	0mg		
sod	64mg		

23% of calories from fat
3% of calories from saturated fat

Freezes well.

WHOLE WHEAT OATMEAL COOKIES

1-1/4 cups whole wheat flour
1/2 tsp baking soda
1/2 tsp cinnamon
1/2 tsp ginger
2 egg whites
1/2 cup unsaturated vegetable oil
1/3 cup brown sugar replacement
1/4 cup honey
1 cup quick oats, uncooked
1/2 cup raisins, cut if desired

In a small bowl, combine flour, baking soda, cinnamon and ginger, set aside. In large mixer bowl, beat egg whites, oil, brown sugar replacement and honey at medium speed until smooth and thick. Add flour mixture and beat until blended. Stir in oats and raisins. Measure heaping teaspoon of mixture and roll into ball. Place balls about 2 inches apart on baking sheet sprayed with release agent. Press balls with floured fork. Bake at 375ºF. 6 to 8 minutes or until edges are browned.

Yield: 4 1/2 dozen cookies

Serves 27.

Per Serving (2 cookies):

Nutrition Information		Exchanges	
cal	88	brd	1/2
pro	1gm	fat	1
carb	11gm		
fat	4gm		
satfat	<1gm		
chol	0mg		
sod	20mg		

40% of calories from fat
6% of calories from saturated fat

Freezes well.

PEANUT BUTTER COOKIES

1 cup Basic Baking Mix (see Index) or Reduced Fat
   Bisquick
6 tab peanut butter
Sweetener to equal 1/3 cup sugar
1/2 tsp vanilla
1/3 cup water or a little more

In large bowl, mix all ingredients together well. Batter will be thick. Drop by teaspoonfuls on cookie sheet sprayed with release agent. To shape cookies, flatten with a fork. Bake at 350°F. about 15 minutes or until done.

Yield: 24 cookies

Serves 24.

Per Serving (1 cookie):

Nutrition Information		Exchanges	
cal	45	brd	1/4
pro	1gm	fat	1/2
carb	4gm		
fat	3gm		
satfat	<1gm		
chol	0mg		
sod	50mg		

60% of calories from fat
10% of calories from saturated fat

Freezes well.

PUMPKIN COOKIES

    2 cups flour
    1 cup quick oats, uncooked
    1 tsp baking soda
    1 tsp cinnamon
    1 tsp ginger
    1 tsp allspice
    1 cup diet imitation margarine
    1 cup brown sugar replacement
    2/3 cup granulated fructose
    2 egg whites
    1 tsp vanilla
    1 cup solid pack pumpkin, no sugar
    1 cup raisins, chopped if desired

Combine flour, oats, baking soda, cinnamon, ginger and allspice and set aside. In large mixer bowl cream margarine, gradually add brown sugar replacement and fructose; beating until light and fluffy. Add egg whites and vanilla. Alternate additions of dry ingredients with pumpkin, mixing well after each addition. Fold in raisins. Drop by teaspoonfuls on cookie sheet sprayed with release agent and spread to desired shape. Bake at 350°F. about 15 minutes or until cookies are lightly browned and firm.

Yield: 80 cookies

Serves 40.

Per Serving (2 cookies):

Nutrition Information		Exchanges	
cal	76	brd	1/2
pro	1gm	fat	1/2
carb	10gm	frt	1/4
fat	<3gm		
satfat	<1gm		
chol	0mg		
sod	76mg		

30% of calories from fat
5% of calories from saturated fat

Freezes well.

SPRITZ COOKIES
(cookie press)

1 cup diet imitation margarine, softened
12 pkts EQUAL or sweetener to equal 1/2 cup sugar
2-1/4 cups all purpose flour (do not use self-rising)
2 egg whites
1 tsp almond or vanilla extract
Food coloring if desired

Heat oven to 400ºF. Cream margarine and sweetener. Blend in rest of ingredients. Fill cookie press with 1/4 of dough at a time and press desired shapes on ungreased cookie sheet. Bake 6 to 9 minutes until set but not brown.

Yield: 5 dozen cookies

Serves 30.

Per Serving (2 cookies):

Nutrition Information		Exchanges	
cal	64	brd	1/2
pro	1gm	fat	1/2
carb	8gm		
fat	3gm		
satfat	<1gm		
chol	0mg		
sod	73mg		

42% of calories from fat
8% of calories from saturated fat

Variations: Before baking, top cookies with raisins, nut pieces or reduced calorie preserves. Adjust calories, etc. if added.

BREAKFASTS

APPLE COFFEE CAKE

2 small apples peeled and thinly sliced
4 slices bread, cubed (see note)
1/2 cup Eggbeaters
2 tsp almond extract
1/2 tsp butter flavoring
1/2 cup evaporated skim milk
1/2 tsp cinnamon
4 egg whites
Sweetner to equal 5 tsp sugar or to taste

Line bottom of 8 X 8 pan, sprayed with release agent, with the sliced apples. Place bread cubes in blender and blend to fine crumbs. Put bread crumbs in mixing bowl, add Eggbeaters and mix well. Add extract, butter flavoring, milk and cinnamon. Mix well. Beat egg whites until stiff, add sweetener, and beat until peaks form. Gently fold egg whites into batter. If desired, sprinkle apples with additional cinnamon and sweetener. Pour batter over apple slices. Bake at 325°F. 45 to 55 minutes or until golden brown.

Serves 4.

Per Serving:

Nutrition Information		Exchanges	
cal	171	pro	1
pro	11gm	brd	1
carb	29gm	fat	1/4
fat	1gm	milk	1/3
satfat	<1gm	frt	3/4
chol	1mg		
sod	263mg		

5% of calories from fat
1% of calories from saturated fat

Note: If using thin bread that is 40 calories per slice, use 6 slices instead of 4.

BAKED CUSTARD PUDDING

1 cup skim milk
1/4 cup Eggbeaters
1 slice white bread, cubed
1 tsp granulated sugar replacement
1/2 tsp vanilla
1/4 tsp cinnamon
1/4 tsp nutmeg

Preheat oven to 350ºF. Combine all ingredients in a medium size bowl. Pour into a 10 ounce custard cup. Bake 20 to 25 minutes or until top is puffed and lightly brown. Serve hot.

Serves 1.

Per Serving:

Nutrition Information		Exchanges	
cal	190	pro	1
pro	15gm	brd	1
carb	27gm	fat	1/4
fat	1gm	milk	1
satfat	<1gm		
chol	4mg		
sod	335mg		

5% of calories from fat
2% of calories from saturated fat

BLUEBERRY MUFFINS

2 slices bread, cubed
1/4 cup Eggbeaters
1 tsp butter flavoring
1/2 tsp almond extract
2 egg whites
Sweetner to equal 2-1/2 tsp sugar, or to taste
1/4 cup blueberries

Put bread cubes into blender and blend to fine crumbs. Put into mixing bowl, add Eggbeaters, flavorings and mix well. Beat egg whites until stiff, add sweetener. Gently fold egg whites into batter, then add blueberries. Pour into muffin tin sprayed with release agent. Makes 6 muffins. Bake 350ºF. 20 to 25 minutes.

Serves 2.

Per Serving (3 muffins):

Nutrition Information		Exchanges	
cal	115	pro	1
pro	8gm	brd	1
carb	17gm	fat	1/4
fat	1gm	frt	1/4
satfat	<1gm		
chol	0mg		
sod	225mg		

8% of calories from fat
2% of calories from saturated fat

Note: If using thin bread that is 40 calories per slice, use 3 slices.

JELLY CHEESE DANISH

1/4 cup part skim ricotta cheese
1/4 tsp vanilla
Dash nutmeg
Dash cinnamon (optional)
1 slice raisin bread, toasted
1 tsp diet jelly (6 calories)

Combine cheese with the vanilla, nutmeg and cinnamon. Spread mixture on toast. Place toast on foil-lined pan. Broil until cheese is hot and bubbly. Remove from oven and top with the jelly.

Serves 1.

Per Serving:

Nutrition Information		Exchanges	
cal	166	pro	1
pro	9gm	brd	1
carb	19gm	fat	3/4
fat	6gm		
satfat	<1gm		
chol	19mg		
sod	171mg		

33% of calories from fat
18% of calories from saturated fat

BREAKFAST DANISH

1 slice whole wheat or white bread
1/3 cup lowfat cottage cheese
Brown sugar replacement
Cinnamon

Toast bread. Spread cottage cheese on toast. Sprinkle with brown sugar and cinnamon. Place toast on foil-lined pan and broil until cheese is hot and bubbly.

Serves 1.

Per Serving (1% milkfat):

Nutrition Information		Exchanges	
cal	118	pro	1
pro	10gm	brd	1
carb	14gm	fat	1/4
fat	<2gm		
satfat	<1gm		
chol	3mg		
sod	405mg		

12% of calories from fat
5% of calories from saturated fat

Per Serving (2% milkfat):

Nutrition Information		Exchanges	
cal	130	pro	1-1/2
pro	12gm	brd	1
carb	15gm	fat	1/4
fat	2gm		
satfat	1gm		
chol	6mg		
sod	405mg		

14% of calories from fat
7% of calories from saturated fat

GRANOLA BREAKFAST BAR

1/4 cup dry oatmeal (not instant)
1 envelope ALBA 77 (vanilla)
1 tsp honey
2 tab raisins
1 tab peanut butter
1 tab cold water

Combine all ingredients and mix thoroughly. Form into a bar on aluminum foil and freeze until firm. Can be stored in freezer or refrigerator. Serve at room temperature.

Serves 1.

Per Serving:

Nutrition Information		Exchanges	
cal	318	pro	1/2
pro	13gm	brd	1
carb	47gm	fat	1-1/2
fat	9gm	milk	1
satfat	<2gm	frt	1
chol	0mg		
sod	229mg		

25% of calories from fat
5% of calories from saturated fat

TOFU FOR BREAKFAST

4 oz tofu
1-1/2 tsp honey
1/4 cup skim milk
Vanilla or almond extract to taste, or both if desired
Cinnamon

Place tofu in saucepan and cover with water. Simmer for 5 minutes, drain. Put tofu, honey, milk and flavorings in blender and blend until smooth. Pour into small bowl, sprinkle with cinnamon and chill.

Note: For best results, make the night before.

Serves 1.

Per Serving:

Nutrition Information   Exchanges

cal   140   pro   1-1/4
pro   11gm   fat   1/3
carb   15gm   milk   1/4
fat   4gm
satfat   0gm
chol   1mg
sod   40mg

26% of calories from fat
0% of calories from saturated fat

Notes:

EGGS / CHEESE

HERB SPINACH BAKE

10 oz pkg frozen chopped spinach, thawed and
   drained
1 cup cooked white rice
1 cup lowfat cheese, grated
3 egg whites, lightly beaten
1/2 cup skim milk
2 tab dried onion flakes
2 tab diet imitation margarine
1/2 tsp Worcestershire sauce
1/2 tsp rosemary, crushed

Combine all ingredients thoroughly. Pour into 8 X 8 baking pan sprayed with release agent. Bake at 350ºF. 20 to 30 minutes or until knife inserted in center comes out clean.

Serves 6.

Per Serving:

Nutrition Information		Exchanges	
cal	118	pro	1
pro	9gm	veg	1/2
carb	13gm	brd	1/2
fat	3gm	fat	1/2
satfat	<1gm		
chol	0mg		
sod	127mg		

23% of calories from fat
3% of calories from saturated fat

COTTAGE CHEESE OMELET

1/4 cup Eggbeaters, lightly beaten, or 1 egg
1 tab water
1/2 tsp chives
1/3 cup lowfat cottage cheese

In a small bowl combine Eggbeaters, water and 1/8 tsp chives. Spray small skillet with release agent. Pour in egg mixture and cook slowly until set. Lift edges as egg mixture cooks, allowing uncooked portion to run under and around cooked sections.

Combine cottage cheese and remaining chives. When omelet is golden on bottom, place cottage cheese mixture on one side of omelet and fold rest of omelet over cottage cheese. Serve immediately.

Serves 1.

With Eggbeaters:

Per Serving (1% milkfat):

Nutrition Information		Exchanges	
cal	74	pro	2
pro	13gm		
carb	3gm		
fat	<1gm		
satfat	<1gm		
chol	3mg		
sod	365mg		

7% of calories from fat
5% of calories from saturated fat

Per Serving (2% milkfat):

Nutrition Information		Exchanges	
cal	86	pro	2-1/2
pro	14gm		
carb	3gm		
fat	1gm		
satfat	<1gm		
chol	6mg		
sod	359mg		

10% of calories from fat
9% of calories from saturated fat

COTTAGE CHEESE OMELET
(continued)

With Egg:

Per Serving (1% milkfat):

Nutrition Information		Exchanges	
cal	124	pro	2
pro	15gm	fat	1/2
carb	3gm		
fat	6gm		
satfat	2gm		
chol	216mg		
sod	·339mg		

44% of calories from fat
14% of calories from saturated fat

Per Serving (2% milkfat):

Nutrition Information		Exchanges	
cal	136	pro	2-1/3
pro	16gm	fat	1/2
carb	3gm		
fat	6gm		
satfat	<3gm		
chol	219mg		
sod	339mg		

40% of calories from fat
16% of calories from saturated fat

HUNGARIAN EGGS

    4 hard cooked eggs
    1/2 cup Eggbeaters
    1/2 cup lowfat cheese, grated (2 oz)
    1 cup plain nonfat yogurt
    2 tsp chopped chives (optional)
    1/2 tsp ground marjoram
    Paprika

Cut the hard cooked eggs in half lengthwise. Remove the yolks being careful not to tear the whites, and throw the yolks away. Cook the Eggbeaters as for scrambled eggs per directions. Using a fork, mash the Eggbeaters until smooth, then mix in 2 tab of yogurt, half the grated cheese and the marjoram. Refill each egg half as for deviled eggs, rejoin the halves firmly.

Place eggs in a shallow baking dish sprayed with release agent. Spread remainder of yogurt over the eggs, sprinkle with rest of grated cheese and color with paprika. Allow to brown in the broiler under a very low flame.

Note: Best when eggs are hard cooked the night before and well chilled. Also very good served cold as deviled eggs.

Serves 4.

With lowfat cheese:

Per Serving:

Nutrition Information		Exchanges	
cal	87	pro	1-1/2
pro	13gm	milk	1/2
carb	6gm		
fat	1gm		
satfat	0gm		
chol	1mg		
sod	138mg		

10% of calories from fat
0% of calories from saturated fat

HUNGARIAN EGGS
(continued)

With Cheddar cheese:

Per Serving:

Nutrition Information		Exchanges	
cal	118	pro	1-1/2
pro	13gm	fat	2/3
carb	5gm	milk	1/2
fat	5gm		
satfat	3gm		
chol	16mg		
sod	226mg		

38% of calories from fat
23% of calories from saturated fat

PUFFY OMELET WITH STRAWBERRIES

2 cups strawberries, sliced
Sweetener to equal 4 tsp sugar
1/2 cup water
4 egg whites
1/2 cup Eggbeaters

Combine strawberries, sweetener and 1/4 cup water. Mix well and set aside.

Preheat oven to 325°F. Beat egg whites and 1/4 cup water with electric mixer on high until stiff and shiny and whites stand in peaks. In a separate bowl, beat Eggbeaters until thick and lemon colored. Lightly fold Eggbeaters into whites. Pour into 10 inch skillet with heatproof handle and sprayed with release agent. Cook about 5 minutes. Place in preheated oven at 325°F. about 15 minutes or until knife inserted in center comes out clean. Serve immediately. Put strawberries on top.

Serves 2.

Note: If using eggs in place of Eggbeaters, use all 4 yolks.

With Eggbeaters:

Per Serving:

Nutrition Information		Exchanges	
cal	108	pro	2
pro	13gm	frt	3/4
carb	13gm		
fat	<1gm		
satfat	0gm		
chol	0mg		
sod	198mg		

4% of calories from fat
0% of calories from saturated fat

PUFFY OMELET
WITH STRAWBERRIES
(continued)

With Eggs:

Per Serving:

Nutrition Information		Exchanges	
cal	199	pro	2
pro	13gm	fat	1
carb	13gm	frt	3/4
fat	11gm		
satfat	3gm		
chol	426mg		
sod	134mg		

50% of calories from fat
14% of calories from saturated fat

EASY QUICHE

1 can crescent rolls (8 oz)
4 oz lowfat Swiss cheese, grated
4 egg whites
1/2 cup Eggbeaters
1 cup skim milk
dash SPIKE or LEMON PEPPER (optional)
Parsley

Spread rolls in bottom of 9 X 13 pan sprayed with release agent. Sprinkle cheese on rolls. Mix egg whites, Eggbeaters and milk together with wire whisk; add seasoning. Pour into pan and sprinkle with parsley. Bake 375°F. for 20 minutes.

Serves 4.

With lowfat cheese:

Per Serving:

Nutrition Information		Exchanges	
cal	301	pro	2
pro	19gm	brd	1-1/2
carb	27gm	fat	2
fat	14gm	milk	1/4
satfat	4gm		
chol	11mg		
sod	587mg		

42% of calories from fat
12% of calories from saturated fat

With regular Swiss cheese:

Per Serving:

Nutrition Information		Exchanges	
cal	347	pro	2
pro	20gm	brd	1-1/2
carb	27gm	fat	3
fat	20gm	milk	1/4
satfat	8gm		
chol	35mg		
sod	979mg		

52% of calories from fat
23% of calories from saturated fat

PINEAPPLE CHEESE QUICHE

    2 cups crushed pineapple with juice, no sugar added
    4 egg whites
    1/2 cup Eggbeaters
    2 cups evaporated skim milk
    4 oz lowfat cheddar cheese, grated

Preheat oven to 425ºF. Lightly beat egg whites and Eggbeaters together. Combine all ingredients and mix well. Spoon mixture into 8 X 8 non-stick baking dish or one that has been sprayed with release agent. Bake at 425ºF. 25 minutes or until set.

Serves 4.

Note: If using eggs in place of Eggbeaters, use all 4 yolks.

With Eggbeaters:

                        Per Serving:
    Nutrition Information   Exchanges

    cal   249   pro   2
    pro   23gm   milk   1-1/3
    carb   34gm   frt   1
    fat   2gm
    satfat   0gm
    chol   5mg
    sod   252mg

7% of calories from fat
0% of calories from saturated fat

With eggs:

                        Per Serving:
    Nutrition Information   Exchanges

    cal   294   pro   2
    pro   23gm   fat   1/2
    carb   34gm   milk   1-1/3
    fat   7gm   frt   1
    satfat   <2gm
    chol   218mg
    sod   220mg

21% of calories from fat
5% of calories from saturated fat

SPINACH QUICHE

2 oz lowfat cheddar cheese grated
6 tab flour
2 tab diet imitation margarine
1/2 cup evaporated skim milk
1/4 cup water
2 tsp dried onion flakes
1/2 cup canned mushrooms, drained and sliced
Dash nutmeg, pepper (optional)
2 egg whites
1/4 cup Eggbeaters
10 oz package frozen spinach, cooked and very well drained

Mix cheese, flour and margarine thoroughly. Press into 8 inch pie pan to form crust. In sauce pan mix milk, water, onion flakes, mushrooms and seasonings. Simmer 1 minute. In another bowl lightly beat egg whites and Eggbeaters, add spinach. Gradually add hot milk mixture. Mix well. Pour into pie pan. Bake at 400°F. 15 minutes, reduce heat to 325°F. and bake additional 25 minutes.

Serves 2.

Note: If using eggs in place of Eggbeaters, use both yolks.

With Eggbeaters:

Per Serving:

Nutrition Information		Exchanges	
cal	322	pro	2
pro	26gm	veg	2-1/3
carb	34gm	brd	1-1/4
fat	8gm	fat	1
satfat	1gm	milk	1/2
chol	1mg		
sod	420mg		

22% of calories from fat
3% of calories from saturated fat

SPINACH QUICHE

(continued)

With eggs:

Per Serving:

Nutrition Information		Exchanges	
cal	367	pro	2
pro	26gm	veg	2-1/3
carb	38gm	brd	1-1/4
fat	14gm	fat	1-1/2
satfat	<3gm	milk	1/2
chol	216mg		
sod	390mg		

34% of calories from fat
7% of calories from saturated fat

QUICK AND EASY PIZZA

1 English muffin
1/2 cup low-sodium tomato sauce
1/8 tsp oregano
1 clove garlic, minced
2 oz lowfat cheese, grated

Toast muffin lightly. Mix tomato sauce, oregano and garlic together. Spread 1/2 of sauce on each muffin half. Put cheese on top. Broil until cheese is melted.

Serves 1.

Per Serving:

Nutrition Information		Exchanges	
cal	309	pro	2
pro	21gm	veg	2-3/4
carb	45gm	brd	2
fat	5gm		
satfat	0gm		
chol	0mg		
sod	440mg		

15% of calories from fat
0% of calories from saturated fat

BREAD / MUFFINS

BASIC BAKING MIX

3 cups flour
4-1/2 tsp baking powder
1/4 tsp cream of tartar
2/3 cup diet imitation margarine

Mix dry ingredients together. Cut in margarine using wire pastry blender. Store refrigerated or in freezer.

Yield: 4 cups.

Per Serving (1 cup):

Nutrition Information		Exchanges	
cal	467	brd	4-3/4
pro	10gm	fat	2-3/4
carb	72gm		
fat	15gm		
satfat	<3gm		
chol	0mg		
sod	695mg		

29% of calories from fat
5% of calories from saturated fat

Note: For variation try different flours or combination of flours (i.e., 2 cups oat flour + 1-1/4 cups rice flour). See Flour Equivalents.

BRAN MUFFINS

1 cup stone ground whole wheat flour
1 tsp baking soda
1-1/2 cups wheat bran (Millers)
1/2 cup raisins, cut in halves or chopped if extra large
2 egg whites or 1/4 cup Eggbeaters
3/4 cup skim milk
2 tab unsaturated vegetable oil
1/2 cup honey

In large bowl, mix together flour, baking soda and bran; add raisins. In small bowl using wire whisk, beat egg whites, Eggbeaters and milk, add oil then honey. Mix thoroughly. Add liquid mixture to dry ingredients, stirring only enough to blend thoroughly. Spoon into muffin tins sprayed with release agent or lined with paper cups (a one ounce scoop is perfect). Bake at 400ºF. for 17 to 20 minutes, until just done to the touch on top of muffin. Do not over cook or muffins will be dry. (Convection oven at 375ºF. for 15 minutes). Makes 15 muffins.

Note: If using eggs in place of Eggbeaters, use 1 whole egg.

With egg whites:

Per Serving (1 muffin):

Nutrition Information		Exchanges	
cal	105	brd	1
pro	4gm	fat	1/2
carb	17gm	frt	1/3
fat	2gm		
satfat	<1gm		
chol	0mg		
sod	71mg		

17% of calories from fat
2% of calories from saturated fat

BRAN MUFFINS
(continued)

With Eggbeaters:

Per Serving (1 muffin):

Nutrition Information		Exchanges	
cal	104	brd	1
pro	4gm	fat	1/2
carb	17gm	frt	1/3
fat	2gm		
satfat	<1gm		
chol	0mg		
sod	69mg		

17% of calories from fat
2% of calories from saturated fat

With whole egg:

Per Serving (1 muffin):

Nutrition Information		Exchanges	
cal	107	brd	1
pro	4gm	fat	1/2
carb	17gm	frt	1/3
fat	<3gm		
satfat	<1gm		
chol	14mg		
sod	68mg		

23% of calories from fat
3% of calories from saturated fat

Freezes well.

Variation: Substitute 2/3 cup oat flour (or 1/3 cup oat flour and 1/2 cup rice flour) for wheat flour and allow muffins to stand 20 minutes before baking.

OAT BRAN MUFFINS

2-1/4 cups oat bran
2 tsp baking powder
1 tsp cinnamon
1/4 cup raisins, cut in halves or chopped if extra large
4 egg whites
3/4 cup skim milk
3/4 cup applesauce
1/3 cup honey

In large bowl, mix together bran, baking powder,cinnamon and raisins. In medium bowl using wire whisk, beat egg whites, and milk; add applesauce then honey. Mix thoroughly. Add liquid mixture to dry ingredients, stirring only enough to blend thoroughly. Let rest 15 to 20 minures. Spoon into muffin tins sprayed with release agent or lined with paper cups (a one ounce scoop is perfect). Bake at 325ºF. for 12 to 15 minutes, until just done to the touch on top of muffin. Do not over cook or muffins will be dry. Makes 18 muffins.

Per Serving (1 muffin):

Nutrition Information		Exchanges	
cal	70	pro	1/3
pro	3gm	brd	2/3
carb	15gm	frt	1/4
fat	<1gm		
satfat	0gm		
chol	0mg		
sod	58mg		

3% of calories from fat
0% of calories from saturated fat

Freezes well.

CRANBERRY CORN MUFFINS

1 package JIFFY corn muffin mix
Whole cranberry sauce made with fructose (i.e., Ocean Spray)

Prepare corn muffins according to directions. Place batter in muffin tins lined with paper cups, filling each cup 2/3 full. Place 1 teaspoon of cranberry sauce on top of each filled cup and swirl lightly through the batter with a toothpick or tip of spoon. Bake according to directions on package. Makes 12 muffins.

Serves 12.

Per Serving (1 muffin):

Nutrition Information		Exchanges	
cal	123	brd	1
pro	3gm	fat	1
carb	19gm		
fat	4gm		
satfat	n/a		
chol	0mg		
sod	242mg		

29% of calories from fat
no data available of calories from saturated fat

PUMPKIN CORNMEAL MUFFINS

1/4 cup diet imitation margarine
1/4 cup honey
2 egg whites, lightly beaten
1/3 cup skim milk
1/2 cup canned pumpkin
1-1/2 cups flour
1/3 cup yellow cornmeal
1 tab baking powder
1/2 tsp cinnamon
1/2 tsp nutmeg

Cream margarine, add honey and beat well. Slowly stir in egg whites, milk and pumpkin. Add rest of ingredients and stir until just moistened. Fill paper lined muffin cups 2/3 full. Bake at 400ºF. 20 to 25 minutes until golden. Makes 12 muffins.

Serves 12.

Per Serving (1 muffin):

Nutrition Information		Exchanges	
cal	118	brd	1
pro	3gm	fat	1/2
carb	22gm		
fat	2gm		
satfat	<1gm		
chol	0mg		
sod	142mg		

15% of calories from fat
3% of calories from saturated fat

Freezes well.

ENGLISH MUFFIN LOAF

6 cups unsifted flour
1 pkg active dry yeast
1 tab granulated fructose
1/4 tsp baking soda
2 cups skim milk
1/2 cup water
Cornmeal

Combine 3 cups flour, yeast, fructose and baking soda. Heat milk and water until very warm (120 - 130ºF.). Add to dry mixture, beating well. Stir in rest of flour. Batter will be stiff. Spoon into 2 8-1/2 X 4-1/2 inch loaf pans that have been sprayed with release agent. and sprinkled with cornmeal. Cover and let rise in a warm place 45 minutes. Bake at 400ºF. for 25 minutes. Remove from pans to cooling rack immediately. Allow to cool completely before slicing.

Yield 2 loaves — 16 slices per loaf.

Serves 32.

Per Serving (1 slice):

Nutrition Information		Exchanges	
cal	93	brd	1-1/4
pro	3gm		
carb	19gm		
fat	0gm		
satfat	0gm		
chol	0mg		
sod	15mg		

0% of calories from fat
0% of calories from saturated fat

EASY BISCUITS

1 cup Basic Baking Mix
1/4 cup skim milk

Mix together and drop by spoonfuls on cookie sheet sprayed with release agent — about 1 inch apart. Bake at 450ºF. for 15 minutes. Makes 8 biscuits.

Serves 4.

Per Serving (2 biscuits):

Nutrition Information		Exchanges	
cal	125	brd	1-1/4
pro	3gm	fat	3/4
carb	19gm		
fat	4gm		
satfat	<1gm		
chol	0mg		
sod	190mg		

29% of calories from fat
5% of calories from saturated fat

PUMPKIN CRANBERRY BREAD

    2-1/4 cups all-purpose flour
    1 tsp allspice
    1 tsp ginger
    1 tsp cinnamon
    1 tsp baking soda
    1 tsp baking powder
    4 egg whites
    1 cup granulated fructose
    1 cup solid pack pumpkin
    2 cups whole cranberry sauce

In large bowl mix together flour, spices, baking soda and baking powder. In medium mixer bowl, beat egg whites, add fructose, pumpkin and cranberry sauce. Pour pumpkin mixture into dry ingredients and stir until moistened. Spoon batter into 2 8x4-inch loaf pans. Bake at 350ºF. 60 minutes or until wooden pick comes out clean. Cool well before slicing. 16 slices per loaf.

Serves 32.

Per Serving (1 slice):

Nutrition Information		Exchanges	
cal	78	brd	1/2
pro	1gm	frt	1/3
carb	14gm		
fat	0gm		
satfat	0gm		
chol	0mg		
sod	38mg		

2% of calories from fat
0% of calories from saturated fat

Freezes well.

COCONUT HONEY BREAD

3 cups flour
1-1/2 tsp baking powder
1-1/2 tsp baking soda
4-1/2 tab shredded unsweetened coconut
4 egg whites
1-1/2 cups skim milk
3/4 cup honey

In a large bowl mix together flour, baking powder, baking soda and coconut. In medium bowl using wire whisk beat egg whites, milk and honey until well blended. Mix liquid mixture and dry ingredients together. Pour into loaf pan sprayed with release agent. Bake at 350ºF. for 50 to 60 minutes, until bread tests done. Makes 1 loaf.

Variation: Bake in miniature muffin tins lined with paper baking cups or sprayed with release agent. Makes 60. Bake at 350ºF. 15 minutes.

Loaf (cut in 16 slices):

Per Serving (1 slice):

Nutrition Information		Exchanges	
cal	155	brd	1-1/4
pro	4gm	fat	1/3
carb	33gm		
fat	1gm		
satfat	<1gm		
chol	0mg		
sod	140mg		

6% of calories from fat
3% of calories from saturated fat

COCONUT HONEY BREAD

(continued)

Mini muffins:

Serves 30.

Per Serving (2 mini muffins):

Nutrition Information		Exchanges	
cal	83	brd	2/3
pro	2gm	fat	1/4
carb	18gm		
fat	<1gm		
satfat	<1gm		
chol	0mg		
sod	75mg		

5% of calories from fat
3% of calories from saturated fat

Note: The miniature muffins are great for Holiday serving and entertaining.

Freezes well.

NUT BREAD

2-1/2 cups flour
1/3 cup granulated fructose
3-1/2 tsp baking powder
2 egg whites
1 cup skim milk
1 cup finely chopped walnuts

Sift flour, fructose and baking powder together. Lightly beat egg whites. Add milk to egg whites and mix. Add flour to liquid and mix thoroughly. Stir in nuts. Pour into loaf pan sprayed with release agent. Let rise 20 minutes. Bake in slow oven at 350ºF. 45 minutes or until done. If using glass baking dish, bake at 325ºF. Let cool before slicing.

Serves 16.

Per Serving (1 slice):

Nutrition Information		Exchanges	
cal	139	pro	1/4
pro	4gm	brd	1
carb	17gm	fat	1
fat	5gm		
satfat	<1gm		
chol	0mg		
sod	90mg		

32% of calories from fat
3% of calories from saturated fat

BANANA NUT BREAD

Prepare Nut Bread as above and add 1 cup mashed ripe bananas (2 - 3).

Serves 16.

Per Serving (1 slice):

Nutrition Information		Exchanges	
cal	152	pro	1/4
pro	4gm	brd	1
carb	21gm	fat	1
fat	5gm	frt	1/4
satfat	<1gm		
chol	0mg		
sod	90mg		

30% of calories from fat
3% of calories from saturated fat

DATE NUT BREAD

Prepare Nut Bread as above and add 1 cup diced dates.

Serves 16.

Per Serving (1 slice):

Nutrition Information		Exchanges	
cal	169	pro	1/4
pro	4gm	brd	1
carb	25gm	fat	1
fat	5gm	frt	2/3
satfat	<1gm		
chol	0mg		
sod	90mg		

27% of calories from fat
2% of calories from saturated fat

PINEAPPLE QUICKBREAD

1/2 cup crushed pineapple, own juice, no sugar added
1/3 cup nonfat dry milk powder
2 egg whites
1 oz dry enriched cornmeal
2 tsp flour
Sweetener to equal 2 tsp sugar
1 tsp baking powder

Preheat oven to 350ºF. Combine all ingredients in blender container and process until mixed but not completely smooth. Line a 6 cup muffin tin or 12 cup miniature muffin tin with paper baking cups and divide mixture evenly into the cups. Bake about 15 minutes or until a toothpick inserted in center comes out dry.

Serves 1.

Per Serving:

Nutrition Information		Exchanges	
cal	307	pro	1
pro	17gm	brd	1-3/4
carb	57gm	milk	1
fat	<1gm	frt	1
satfat	0gm		
chol	4mg		
sod	575mg		

2% of calories from fat
0% of calories from saturated fat

ZUCCHINI BREAD

3 cups flour
2 tsp cinnamon
1 tsp baking soda
1/4 tsp baking powder
1/2 cup walnuts, chopped
1 cup raisins, chopped
4 egg whites
1/4 cup Eggbeaters
2/3 cup unsaturated vegetable oil
3/4 cup granulated sugar replacement
3/4 cup brown sugar replacement
1 tsp vanilla
1/4 cup nonfat dry milk powder
2 cups peeled and grated zucchini

In bowl combine flour, cinnamon, baking soda and powder, walnuts and raisins. In large bowl beat egg whites, Eggbeaters, both sugar replacements and vanilla. Gradually add oil and continue beating until well blended. Add dry milk powder and mix thoroughly. Using wooden spoon for the balance of mixing, add the grated zucchini and dry ingredients. Batter is thick.

Pour into 2 loaf pans that have been sprayed with release agent and lightly floured. Bake at 325ºF. for 2 hours. Allow to cool completely before slicing.

Yield: 2 loaves — 16 slices per loaf.

Serves 32.

Per Serving (1 slice):

Nutrition Information		Exchanges	
cal	115	pro	1/2
pro	3gm	fat	1
carb	14gm	frt	1/4
fat	5gm		
satfat	<1gm		
chol	0mg		
sod	42mg		

39% of calories from fat
1% of calories from saturated fat

Freezes well.

Notes:

BEVERAGES

STRAWBERRY COOLER

1 cup skim milk
1 cup crushed ice
1 pkt EQUAL or to taste
1/2 cup strawberries
1/2 tsp lemon juice (optional)
Dash nutmeg

Place all ingredients in blender except nutmeg. Process until smooth. Pour into a tall glass and sprinkle with nutmeg.

Serves 1.

Per Serving:

Nutrition Information		Exchanges	
cal	112	milk	1
pro	9gm	frt	1/2
carb	18gm		
fat	1gm		
satfat	<1gm		
chol	4mg		
sod	127mg		

8% of calories from fat
2% of calories from saturated fat

BANANA COOLER

1 cup skim milk
1 cup crushed ice
1 pkt EQUAL or to taste
1/2 medium banana sliced
1/4 tsp vanilla

Combine all ingredients in blender. Process until smooth. Pour into a tall chilled glass.

Serves 1.

Per Serving:

Nutrition Information		Exchanges	
cal	146	milk	1
pro	9gm	frt	1
carb	27gm		
fat	1gm		
satfat	<1gm		
chol	4mg		
sod	127mg		

6% of calories from fat
2% of calories from saturated fat

COCONUT COOLER

1-1/2 cups skim milk
3/4 tsp coconut extract
1/4 tsp rum extract
2 pkts EQUAL or to taste
10 ice cubes

In blender combine skim milk, extracts and EQUAL. Blend on high about 30 seconds. Add ice cubes one at a time, blending after each addition until smooth and mixture is thickened. Spoon into dessert dishes and serve at once.

Serves 2.

Per Serving:

Nutrition Information		Exchanges	
cal	75	milk	3/4
pro	6gm		
carb	11gm		
fat	0gm		
satfat	0gm		
chol	3mg		
sod	95mg		

0% of calories from fat
0% of calories from saturated fat

ORANGE DELITE

3/4 cup skim milk
1/4 cup orange juice
1 tsp vanilla
1 pkt EQUAL or to taste
2 to 4 ice cubes

Combine all ingredients except ice cubes in blender and process about 30 seconds. Add ice cubes one at a time and process until smooth.

Serves 1.

Per Serving:

Nutrition Information		Exchanges	
cal	110	milk	3/4
pro	7gm	frt	1/2
carb	18gm		
fat	0gm		
satfat	0gm		
chol	3mg		
sod	95mg		

0% of calories from fat
0% of calories from saturated fat

MILKSHAKE

1 cup skim milk
1/2 to 3/4 tsp extract, any flavor
Sweetener to taste
3 ice cubes

Place all ingredients except ice cubes in blender and process about 15 seconds. Add ice cubes one at a time blending until frothy.

Serves 1.

Per Serving:

Nutrition Information		Exchanges	
cal	97	milk	1
pro	8gm		
carb	14gm		
fat	0gm		
satfat	0gm		
chol	4mg		
sod	126mg		

0% of calories from fat
0% of calories from saturated fat

PINEAPPLE SHAKE

3/4 cup lowfat buttermilk
1/2 cup crushed pineapple, own juice no sugar added
Sweetener to taste
3 ice cubes

Combine all ingredients except ice cubes in blender and process about 30 seconds. Add ice cubes one at a time and process until smooth.

Serves 1.

Per Serving:

Nutrition Information		Exchanges	
cal	152	fat	1/2
pro	6gm	milk	3/4
carb	29gm	frt	1
fat	<2gm		
satfat	1gm		
chol	7mg		
sod	203mg		

9% of calories from fat
6% of calories from saturated fat

BUTTERMILK PICK-ME-UP

3 cups cold lowfat buttermilk
1/2 cup orange juice
2-1/2 tab lemon juice
4 pkts EQUAL or to taste
3/4 tsp grated lemon rind

Combine all ingredients in blender. Blend on medium about 30 seconds. Chill before serving.

Serves 4.

Per Serving:

Nutrition Information		Exchanges	
cal	92	fat	1/2
pro	6gm	milk	3/4
carb	13gm	frt	1/4
fat	<2gm		
satfat	1gm		
chol	7mg		
sod	193mg		

16% of calories from fat
10% of calories from saturated fat

TROPICAL CRUSH

1/2 medium banana, sliced
1/2 cup crushed pineapple, own juice no sugar added
1 cup diet ginger ale, cold

Combine banana and crushed pineapple in blender and process
until smooth. Add ginger ale and process about 30 seconds or
until combined. Serve in a chilled glass.

Serves 2.

Per Serving:

Nutrition Information		Exchanges	
cal	6	frt	1
pro	0gm		
carb	16gm		
fat	0gm		
satfat	0gm		
chol	0mg		
sod	13mg		

0% of calories from fat
0% of calories from saturated fat

HOLIDAY NOG

2/3 cup water
1/3 cup nonfat dry milk powder
1 pkt EQUAL or to taste
1/2 tsp brandy extract
1/2 tsp vanilla
Dash ground nutmeg
3 ice cubes

Combine all ingredients except ice cubes in blender. Process until frothy. Add ice cubes one at a time, blending after each addition until very thick. Pour into a chilled glass.

Serves 1.

Per Serving:

Nutrition Information		Exchanges	
cal	86	milk	1
pro	7gm		
carb	12gm		
fat	0gm		
satfat	0gm		
chol	4mg		
sod	116mg		

0% of calories from fat
0% of calories from saturated fat

EGGNOG

1 cup skim milk
2 egg whites
1 pkt EQUAL
1/4 tsp cinnamon
1/8 tsp nutmeg
1/4 tsp vanilla

Place all ingredients in blender. Process until frothy. Pour into a tall glass. Serve at once.

Serves 1.

Note: Can use in place of egg whites: 1/4 cup Eggbeaters or 1 whole egg.

With egg whites:

Per Serving:

Nutrition Information		Exchanges	
cal	131	pro	1
pro	15gm	milk	1
carb	15gm		
fat	<1gm		
satfat	<1gm		
chol	4mg		
sod	236mg		

3% of calories from fat
2% of calories from saturated fat

With Eggbeaters (1/4 cup):

Per Serving:

Nutrition Information		Exchanges	
cal	121	pro	1
pro	13gm	milk	1
carb	15gm		
fat	<1gm		
satfat	<1gm		
chol	4mg		
sod	206mg		

4% of calories from fat
3% of calories from saturated fat

EGGNOG

(continued)

With whole egg:

Per Serving:

Nutrition Information		Exchanges	
cal	171	pro	1
pro	15gm	fat	1/2
carb	14gm	milk	1
fat	6gm		
satfat	2gm		
chol	217mg		
sod	189mg		

29% of calories from fat
10% of calories from saturated fat

HOT MOCHA

1 tsp instant decaf coffee
1/3 cup nonfat dry milk powder
1 pkt EQUAL or to taste
1-1/2 to 2 tsp vanilla
1 cup boiling water

Combine all ingredients in blender and process about 30 seconds.
Serve warm.

Serves 1.

Per Serving:

Nutrition Information		Exchanges	
cal	98	milk	1
pro	7gm		
carb	14gm		
fat	0gm		
satfat	0gm		
chol	4mg		
sod	120mg		

0% of calories from fat
0% of calories from saturated fat

BRANDY ALEXANDER

1/3 cup nonfat dry milk powder
1/2 cup diet cream soda
1/2 tsp brandy extract
2 ice cubes

Combine all ingredients except ice cubes in blender and process about 30 seconds. Add ice cubes one at a time blending after each addition. Serve in chilled stemmed glass.

Serves 1.

Per Serving:

Nutrition Information		Exchanges	
cal	80	milk	1
pro	7gm		
carb	11gm		
fat	0gm		
satfat	0gm		
chol	4mg		
sod	120mg		

0% of calories from fat
0% of calories from saturated fat

WHISKEY SOUR

    1 capful pure cherry extract
    1 capful rum or brandy extract
    1/2 cup orange juice
    1/4 cup lime juice
    1/2 cup cold water
    1 pkt EQUAL or to taste
    4 ice cubes

Combine all ingredients except ice cubes in blender and process on medium about 30 seconds. Add ice cubes one at a time blending after each addition.

Serves 1.

Per Serving:

Nutrition Information		Exchanges	
cal	87	frt	1-1/4
pro	1gm		
carb	20gm		
fat	0gm		
satfat	0gm		
chol	0mg		
sod	14mg		

0% of calories from fat
0% of calories from saturated fat

PINK LADY

1 cup skim milk
1 capful rum extract
1 pkt EQUAL or to taste
1 drop red food coloring
2 ice cubes

Combine all ingredients except ice cubes in blender and process about 20 seconds. Add ice cubes one at a time blending after each addition until smooth. Serve in a stemmed glass.

Serves 1.

Per Serving:

Nutrition Information		Exchanges	
cal	94	milk	1
pro	8gm		
carb	13gm		
fat	0gm		
satfat	0gm		
chol	4mg		
sod	126mg		

0% of calories from fat
0% of calories from saturated fat

Notes:

INDEX

INDEX

Ambrosia Pie, 123
Ambrosia Whip, 94
Angel Clouds, 97
Appetizers and Snacks
  Banana Chips, 34
  Carob Peanut Butter Cups, 33
  Citrus Snacks, 31
  Coconut Peanut Butter Balls, 35
  Crabmeat Ball, 23
  Creamy Tofu Dip, 26
  Date Balls, 30
  Gelatin Snacks, 32
  Guacamole, 37
  Hummus, 27
  Oriental Dip, 25
  Sardine Spread, 24
  Sour Cream (Cottage Cheese), 38
  Stuffed Dates, 29
  Stuffed Zucchini Rounds, 28
  Veggie Dip, 36
Apple Coffee Cake, 141
Apple Pie, 122
Applesauce Cookies, 133
Apricot Upside-down Cake, 109

Baked Apple, 92
Baked Custard Pudding, 142
Banana Chips, 34
Banana Cooler, 178
Banana Cream Pie I, 124
Banana Cream Pie II, 125
Banana Nut Bread, 173
Basic Baking Mix, 161
Beverages
  Banana Cooler, 178
  Brandy Alexander, 189
  Buttermilk Pick-Me-Up, 183
  Coconut Cooler, 179
  Eggnog, 186
  Holiday Nog, 185
  Hot Mocha, 188
  Milkshake, 181
  Orange Delite, 180
  Pineapple Shake, 182
  Pink Lady, 191
  Strawberry Cooler, 177
  Tropical Crush, 184
  Whiskey Sour, 190
Blueberry Muffins, 143
Bran Muffins, 162
Brandy Alexander, 189

Breads
  Banana Nut, 173
  Coconut Honey, 170
  Date Nut, 173
  English Muffin Loaf, 167
  Nut, 172
  Pineapple Quickbread, 174
  Pumpkin Cranberry, 169
  Zucchini, 175
Breakfasts
  Apple Coffee Cake, 141
  Baked Custard Pudding, 142
  Blueberry Muffins, 143
  Danish, 145
  Granola Breakfast Bar, 146
  Jelly Cheese Danish, 144
  Tofu For Breakfast, 147
Breakfast Danish, 145
Brownies, 134
Buttermilk Pick-Me-Up, 183

Cakes
  Apricot Upside-down, 109
  Carrot, 114
  Fruit, 116
  Fruit Cocktail, 113
  Fruited Cheesecake, 110
  Pina Colada, 118
  Plain Cheesecake, 111
  Pumpkin, 119
  Quick and Easy Cheesecake, 112
Calculating Fat Percent in Food, 5
Carob Chip Cookies, 135
Carob Peanut Butter Cups, 33
Carrot Cake, 114
Chicken
  Dijon, 59
  Egg Rolls, 61
  Kabobs, 57
  Salad, 49
  Teriyaki, 58
Chicken Dijon, 59
Chicken Kabobs, 57
Chicken Salad, 49
Chicken Teriyaki, 58
Chocolate Mint Freeze, 96
Citrus Snacks, 31
Coconut Cooler, 179
Coconut Honey Bread, 170
Coconut Peanut Butter Balls, 35

INDEX
(continued)

Cookies
    Applesauce, 133
    Brownies, 134
    Carob Chip, 135
    Oatmeal, 136
    Peanut Butter, 138
    Pumpkin, 139
    Spritz, 140
    Whole Wheat Oatmeal, 137
Cottage Cheese Omelet, 150
Crabmeat Ball, 23
Crabmeat Melt, 60
Cranberry Chutney, 53
Cranberry Corn Muffins, 165
Cream Cheese Frosting, 120
Creamy Tofu Dip, 26
Cucumber Salad Dressing, 52

Date Balls, 30
Date Nut Bread, 173
Dedication, 3
Deep Dish Apple Pie, 121
Desserts
    Ambrosia Whip, 94
    Angel Clouds, 97
    Baked Apple, 92
    Chocolate Mint Freeze, 96
    Dreamy Fruit, 93
    Mousse, 91
    Orange Whip, 95
    Peach Cobbler, 103
    Pineapple Cheese Baklava, 100
    Pineapple Delite, 98
    Pineapple Fluff, 99
    Pumpkin Pineapple Pudding, 105
    Rice Pudding, 104
    Strawberry Cobbler, 102
    Strawberry Pudding, 106
    Trifle, 107
Dreamy Fruit, 93

Easy Biscuits, 168
Easy Quiche, 156
Egg Rolls, 61
Eggnog, 186
Eggplant Italian Style, 62
Eggplant Mid-east Style, 63
Eggs and Cheese
    Cottage Cheese Omelet, 150
    Easy Quiche, 156
    Herb Spinach Bake, 149
    Hungarian Eggs, 152
    Lasagna Florentine, 74
    Pineapple Cheese Quiche, 157
    Puffy Omelet with Strawberries, 154
    Quick and Easy Pizza, 160
    Spinach Quiche, 158
English Muffin Loaf, 167

Fish
    Crabmeat Melt, 60
    Orange Glazed, 64
    Poached, 65
    Polynesian, 67
    Salmon Roast BBQ, 79
    Teryiaki, 66
Fish and Fruit Salad, 46
Flour Equivalents, 15
Food Groups, 4
French Dressing, 54
Fruit Cake, 116
Fruit Cocktail Cake, 113
Fruited Cheesecake, 110

Garbanzo Burgers, 69
Gelatin Snacks, 32
Graham Cracker Crust, 111
Granola Breakfast Bar, 146
Guacamole, 37

Helpful Hints, 10
Herb Spinach Bake, 149
Holiday Carrots, 42
Holiday Nog, 185
Homemade Egg Substitute, 16
Honey-Mustard Dressing, 55
Hot Mocha, 188
How Recipes Are Analyzed, 4
Hummus, 27
Hungarian Eggs, 152

Italian Tuna Pie, 70
Jelly Cheese Danish, 144

Kibbee Baked, 71
Kibbee Baked Stuffed, 72
Lasagna Florentine, 74

Mexican Style Meatloaf, 78
Mexican Bean Casserole, 77

INDEX
(continued)

Milkshake, 181
Mousse, 91
Muffins
    Bran, 162
    Cranberry Corn, 165
    Oat Bran, 164
    Pumpkin Cornmeal, 166

Nut Bread, 172
Nutritional Information, 4

Oat Bran Muffins, 164
Oatmeal Cookies, 136
Orange Delite, 180
Orange Glazed Fish, 64
Orange Whip, 95
Oranged Squash, 44
Oriental Dip, 25

Peach Cobbler, 103
Peanut Butter Cookies, 138
Pies
    Ambrosia, 123
    Apple, 122
    Banana Cream I, 124
    Banana Cream II, 125
    Deep Dish Apple, 121
    Pineapple, 129
    Pistachio, 126
    Pumpkin Chiffon, 132
    Pumpkin, 130
    Strawberry Glaze, 127
    Strawberry, 128
Pina Colada Cake, 118
Pineapple Cheese Baklava, 100
Pineapple Cheese Quiche, 157
Pineapple Delite, 98
Pineapple Fluff, 99
Pineapple Pie, 129
Pineapple Quickbread, 174
Pineapple Shake, 182
Pink Lady, 191
Pistachio Pie, 126
Plain Cheesecake, 111
Poached Fish, 65
Polynesian Fish, 67
Powdered Sugar Replacement, 14
Preface, 1
Products Used, 17
Puffy Omelet with Strawberries, 154

Pumpkin Cake, 119
Pumpkin Cranberry Bread, 169
Pumpkin Chiffon Pie, 132
Pumpkin Cookies, 139
Pumpkin Cornmeal Muffins, 166
Pumpkin Pie, 130
Pumpkin Pineapple Pudding, 105

Quiche
    Easy, 156
    Pineapple Cheese, 157
    Spinach, 158
Quick and Easy Cheesecake, 112
Quick and Easy Pizza, 160
Rice Pudding, 104

Salad Dressings
    Cucumber, 52
    French, 54
    Honey-Mustard, 55
Salads
    Chicken, 49
    Fish and Fruit, 46
    Southwest Rice, 48
    Sweet and Sour Cole Slaw, 50
    Tuna, 51
    Waldorf, 47
Salmon Roast BBQ, 79
Sample Menus, 19
Sardine Spread, 24
Scalloped Tuna, 80
Sour Cream (Cottage Cheese), 38
Southwest Rice Salad, 48
Spaghetti Squash Casserole, 43
Spicy Tuna Casserole, 81
Spinach Pie, 40
Spinach Puffs, 39
Spinach Quiche, 158
Spritz Cookies, 140
Strawberry Cobbler, 102
Strawberry Cooler, 177
Strawberry Glaze Pie, 127
Strawberry Pie, 128
Strawberry Pudding, 106
Stuffed Dates, 29
Stuffed Grape Leaves, 68
Stuffed Zucchini, 89
Stuffed Zucchini Rounds, 28
Substitutions, 16

INDEX
(continued)

Sugar Equivalents, 14
Sweet and Sour Cole Slaw, 50

Teryiaki Fish, 66
Teryiaki Marinade, 56
Tofu For Breakfast, 147
Tofu Stir Fry, 76
Trifle, 107
Tropical Crush, 184
Tuna
  Italian Tuna Pie, 70
  Loaf, 82
  Mushroom Diablo, 83
  Salad, 51
  Scalloped, 80
  Spicy Casserole, 81
  Stuffed Peppers, 84
Tuna Loaf, 82
Tuna Mushroom Diablo, 83
Tuna Salad, 51
Tuna Stuffed Peppers, 84
Turkey
  Burgers, 85
  Divan, 86
  Eggplant Italian Style, 62
  Eggplant Mid-east Style, 63
  Kibbee Baked, 71
  Kibbee Baked Stuffed, 72
  Loaf I, 87
  Loaf II, 88
  Mexican Style Meatloaf, 78
  Stuffed Grape Leaves, 68
  Stuffed Zucchini, 89
Turkey Burgers, 85
Turkey Divan, 86
Turkey Loaf I, 87
Turkey Loaf II, 88

Vegetables
  Garbanzo Burgers, 69
  Holiday Carrots, 42
  Mexican Bean Casserole, 77
  Oranged Squash, 44
  Spaghetti Squash Casserole, 43
  Spinach Pie, 40
  Spinach Puffs, 39
  Tofu Stir Fry, 76
  Zucchini and Onions, 45
Veggie Dip, 36

Waldorf Salad, 47
Weights and Measures, 13
What Labels Really Mean, 7
Whipped Cream Substitute, 131
Whiskey Sour, 190
Whole Wheat Oatmeal Cookies, 137
Zucchini and Onions, 45
Zucchini Bread, 175